DICTIONARY OF
PERSONAL COMPUTING
AND
THE INTERNET

S.M.H. Collin

FITZROY DEARBORN PUBLISHERS
CHICAGO • LONDON

FITZROY DEARBORN PUBLISHERS
70 East Walton Street
Chicago, Illinois 60611
USA

or

11 Rathbone Place
London W1P 1DE
England

Library of Congress and British Library Cataloging in Publication Data is available.

ISBN 1-57958-016-5

First published in the USA and UK 1997

Typeset by PCP
Printed in Great Britain by Butler and Tanner

Cover: Peter Aristedes, Chicago Advertising and Design

PREFACE

Over the past two years, the internet has grown at an astonishing rate. Almost everyone has heard about it and an increasing number of people use it regularly. There are estimated to be over 30 million people connected, in some way, to the internet – whether they know it or not. Much of the enthusiasm for the internet has come from the easy access to cheap, powerful personal computers that allow small companies to set up on the internet and provide just as good a service as their larger competitors.

If you are trying to understand PC technology and the internet, you are in an area that has more jargon and acronyms than just about any other technical subject. New products and technologies are launched regularly and would amaze any user of the original simple IBM PC that launched the personal computer revolution.

In this dictionary I have tried to cover all the areas that include complex jargon and confusing terms: from the components that make up a PC, the way they work, to the software that they run. If you want to upgrade your PC, you will enter an equally complex area, with different types of memory, hard disks and network cards. If you want to connect to the internet, you will also have to understand communications jargon and modern technology. To get the most from the internet, you will need to look at the many different ways in which you can use it – including electronic mail, transferring files and the world wide web. Lastly, for competent users, you should create your own web page – using HTML commands that are covered in the appendix at the end of this dictionary.

This dictionary is aimed at any user who wants to understand the complex terms that are used to describe PCs and the internet. I have included clear definitions for all of the terms, and added notes and examples for many of the more important terms. If you are a student, new computer user or new to the internet, you should find this dictionary useful.

Aa

A:

letter that is used in some operating systems, including DOS, Windows and OS/2 and that denotes the first disk drive on the system. Normally, a PC has two or three disk drives within its casing. One floppy disk, called 'A:' and one hard disk called 'C:'. If you have a second floppy disk, this is called 'B:' and a CD-ROM drive is normally 'D:'. When talking about the different disk drives, you say 'Drive A' for the floppy drive, but normally write 'A:'. If you are using DOS, when your PC starts up it will normally show what's called the C-prompt (which looks like 'C:\>' on your screen); this means you are currently looking at the hard disk. If you want to change to drive A to read data from a floppy disk, enter 'A:' and press return.

see also
C:, FLOPPY DISK, HARD DISK

acceleration

see
MOUSE ACCELERATION

accelerator, accelerator key

combination of keys that, when pressed together, carry out a function that would otherwise have to be selected from a menu using a mouse. For example, instead of selecting the File menu then the Save option, many programs let you use the accelerator keys Alt and S to do the same thing and save the file.

accelerator card

method of speeding up an old PC by replacing the existing processor with a special add-in card that has a newer, faster processor. Accelerator cards are not really recommended unless you have no other way of upgrading your PC. The main problem is that although you replace the processor, you are still using the original, old memory and disks. Accelerator cards are also notoriously sensitive and can cause problems for no apparent reason. In short, try and use other methods of improving the speed of your PC: use disk caching software or add more memory.

see also
UPGRADE

acceptable use policy

see
AUP

access

to use something, such as a shared resource on a network

access provider

see

ISP

access time

time taken to find and retrieve a particular piece of data from memory or a hard disk. If you are adding more memory (RAM) to your PC, you have to make sure that you buy chips or SIMMs that are at least as fast as the existing ones. Memory chips have an access time of around 100nano-seconds. However, access time is normally used for hard disks as a way of giving some idea of the hard disk's performance. With hard disks, the average access time is often quoted. Measured in thousandths of a second (ms), this is the time it typically takes for the drive to get to a sector of the disk after the computer has requested that particular sector. If you have a PC with an 80386 or 80486 processor, you should make sure that the hard disk has a maximum access time of around 20-25ms.

account

If you are connected to a network within your office, or if you use a bulletin board or electronic mail system, then you have a personal account. Rather like your bank account, this has a password that only you know, together with an account name that identifies you. You account will also hold records of your rights to access parts of the network and will store any electronic mail that you receive. If you are a new user on the network, you will have to ask the supervisor to create an account for you.

accounting

popular software application for automating accounting and book-keeping

acoustic coupler

type of modem that has rubber cups that fit around the mouth and ear-piece of a normaltelephone handset. This converts data from the computer into sound that is then transmitted across the telephone network to another computer with a modem. Most modems plug directly into a telephone socket and provide better quality sound which means that they are more reliable when sending data. An acoustic coupler sends data more slowly than a modem plugged directly into the phone socket, but it is very useful if you are travelling and need to use public or hotel phones to send data.

Acrobat™

see

ADOBE ACROBAT

acronym

abbreviation, formed from various letters, which makes up a word which can be pronounced. For example, the acronym RAM means Random Access Memory.

active matrix display

type of colour display used in laptop computers normally called TFT display; provides a clear, crisp display but is more expensive than a passive matrix display (often called STN)

see also

TFT

active window

active window

section of a screen that is currently being used. In Microsoft Windows, the active
window is in front of any other windows and has its title bar (at the top of the
window) coloured blue (windows which are displayed but are not active have a
white title bar).

ActiveVRML™

see
VRML

ActiveX™

programming language and program definition used to create small applications
designed to enhance the functionality of a Web page; for example, if you want to
add multimedia effects to your Web page, you cannot carry out these functions with
standard HTML commands, so you could write a small ActiveX program, called an
applet, that is automatically downloaded by the user's browser and runs on the
user's computer
see also
APPLET, JAVA, VBSCRIPT

adapter, adapter card

card that plugs into an expansion bus in a PC and adds a new function to the
computer, or allows it to communicate with another device. For example, a sound
card is a type of adapter card that plugs into an expansion connector and allows
sound to be played back or recorded.

add-on, add-in

device that connects to a computer, more properly called a peripheral. 'Add-in' is
sometimes used to distinguish devices which fit inside the computer rather than
plug into it. Some software packages are designed to allow 'add-on' or 'add-in'
modules to be purchased that enhance the original program.

address

i) unique number that identifies a particular storage location in a computer's
memory. Each location can store one byte of data (that's eight bits) and most PCs
have 4Mb of main memory - that's four million separate addresses. Other parts of a
computer system are often identified by numbers or addresses. For example, in a
network, each PC typically has its own network or station address, a unique number
that identifies it to other machines on the network.
ii) (on the internet) unique series of numbers that identifies your Web server or
domain; for example, 152.222.33.2 might be the address of a Web server, but it is
normally written using characters, for example www.pcp.co.uk is the name address
of the Peter Collin Publishing Web server. When you want to access a page stored
on a Web server, you enter the name address in your Web browser, this passes the

name to a DNS computer that looks up this name in a table and finds the correct numeric address and so can find the Web server.

iii) (in electronic mail) unique combination of a user's name and domain name that identifies you to other users; for example, if you want to send electronic mail to Peter Collin Publishing, you would use the unique address 'info@pcp.co.uk'. The part to the right of the '@' symbol is called the domain, type of organisation and country, the part to the left of the '@' symbol identifies the user at the company or domain
see also
DOMAIN

address book

list of network or internet users and their electronic mail address, used with an electronic mail application to simplify sending mail to a user - you can select the user's name from the address book rather than enter their full email address

address bus

set of electrical lines between the computer's processor and the storage devices. The bus normally has 24 or 32 separate lines to select any one of the millions of possible addresses; the addresses are selected by the processor. The number of lines in the address bus - also called its size or width - dictates how much memory can be accessed directly. An impractical example is a 2-wire (or 2-bit) address bus which can only access four memory locations, corresponding to off-off, off-on, on-off and on-on. Old 8-bit micros typically used a 16-bit address bus, providing access to 65536 (64K) separate locations in memory. A PC or XT micro (one with an 8088 or 8086 chip) has a 20-bit address bus, allowing up to 1Mb of memory. An 80286 adds four further lines, allowing up to 16Mb of memory (each additional line doubles the number of different combinations that can be sent out).
see also
BIT, DATA BUS

Adobe Type Manager™ (ATM)

software standard that is used to describe the shape of fonts and how they can be re-sized to almost any size without changing the quality. This standard is used with Apple System 7 and Microsoft Windows 3.1 to display fonts that can be scaled to almost any point size, and printed on almost any printer. Adobe is a software company that developed products including Acrobat, ATM, and PostScript.

Adobe Acrobat™

software that converts documents and formatted pages into a file format that can be viewed on almost any computer platform or using a Web browser on the internet; for example, if you publish a newsletter, you could lay out the pages using a desktop publish system, print the pages for a paper version and convert the files to Acrobat format allowing you to distribute the same pages on CD-ROM or on the internet

agent

software that will search the internet for particular information; agents automate the work of using several search indexes

AI

ARTIFICIAL INTELLIGENCE
design and development of computer programs that attempt to imitate human intelligence and decision-making functions, providing basic reasoning and other human characteristics.

algorithm
method or procedure that solves a particular problem or performs some desired task. Programmers write instructions to implement particular algorithms in their programs. The choice of algorithm affects performance, memory requirements and so forth. For example, some methods of sorting are very quick while others are slower but do not need as much memory or disk space to operate.

alias
simple name for a user or group of users, interpreted by email software. Using an alias means you don't have to remember complicated mail addresses.

align
to line up text so that either the left or right-hand margin is level. If text is left-aligned, all the characters line up on the left hand side, but don't on the right-hand side. If text is justified then the text lines up on both the left and right-hand edges.

Alpha™
processor chip developed by Digital Equipment Corp. that provides high-speed computing power; the Alpha chip is a 64-bit processor that uses RISC architecture

alt
type of newsgroup on the internet that contains discussions about alternative subjects; these are not official newsgroups and are not supported or monitored by any company, and any user can write just about anything that they want to say. Some of the larger online service providers do not allow their subscribers to view all of the alt newsgroups because they may contain offensive and pornographic material

Alt key
key on a PC keyboard used to activate special functions in an application. The Alt key has become the standard method of activating a menu bar in any software running on a PC; for example, Alt-F normally displays the File menu of a program, Alt-X normally exits the program.

America Online™ (AOL)
largest online service provider in the world, with over eight million subscribers. The company provides access to the internet and provides databases of information that can only be accessed by its subscribers
see also
COMPUSERVE

amplitude
voltage level or size of a signal; for example, a loud sound has a large amplitude

analog monitor
monitor that accepts analog video signals and so can display an almost infinite range of colours. Both VGA and S-VGA monitors are analog, wheras the older CGA and EGA monitors are digital and can only display a limited range of colours.

analog to digital conversion (ADC)
electronic circuit that converts an analog signal (such as a sound signal from a microphone) into a numeric form. It does this by looking at the height of the analog signal thousands of times every second (a process called sampling) and storing the height as a stream of numbers.

analog *or* analogue

signal whose value can vary continuously over time rather than taking a fixed values. For example, when someone speaks, the sound wave is an analog signal; it varies smoothly as the person speaks. In contrast, a gear box is a digital device; a car can be in first, second, third or reverse but not in 'first-and-a-half'. PCs will only work with numbers so cannot directly deal with analog signals. To get around this, you need to fit an analog-to-digital converter (A/D converter). For example, a sound card contains an Analog to digital converter to convert the sound signal from the microphone into numbers representing the volume.

AND

operator (often used in searches) that matches text that contains both search words; for example, searching for 'cat AND dog' finds all entries that contain both the words 'cat' and 'dog'
compare with
OR

animated GIF

way of saving several small graphic images within one file so that they can be repeatedly displayed in sequence giving an impression of animation; often used to create animated buttons or other effects on a Web page

animation software

software that allows you to draw several separate frames, each slightly different, and then display them one after another in rapid succession to give the impression of movement. Each frame is called a cel and the objects that move are normally called actors.

anonymous FTP

method commonly used on the internet that allows a user to connect to a remote computer using the FTP protocol and log in as a guest to download publicly accessible files; if you are using the FTP protocol to connect to a remote computer and you are asked for a login name and password, you can normally gain access to the remote computer's public areas by entering 'anonymous' as the login user name and your full email address as the password
see also
FTP

ANSI

AMERICAN NATIONAL STANDARDS INSTITUTE
American organisation that produces various formal standards for the computer industry. ANSI is best known to PC users for its screen control standard which is provided with DOS in the form of ANSI.SYS.

ANSI.SYS

(software) device driver that is supplied with DOS and allows programs to use a series of special character sequences to change the colour and position of characters displayed on screen. ANSI.SYS also provides extra controls for the keyboard and is normally used within batch files to enhance the look of a program. If you want to experiment with ANSI.SYS, it must be loaded when the PC is started by adding a line such as 'DEVICE=\DOS\ANSI.SYS' to the CONFIG.SYS file on the disk used to start the PC. It is easy to spot if a program needs ANSI.SYS when ANSI.SYS is not loaded since the special character sequences will appear on the screen rather than being carried out, leaving the screen display unreadable (no harm is done).

These sequences show up as a left arrow, left square bracket and then a combination of letters and numbers. If ANSI.SYS is not required, it is best not to load it since it takes up memory. However, you may want to load it to customise your keyboard and screen. To do this, you need to send one or more ANSI sequences to the screen (some common ones are listed in the table). This can be done by creating a text file containing the relevant codes or using a program especially written for the purpose. It's also possible to use the PROMPT command. For example, the command PROMPT $e[33;42;m;$n$g tells ANSI.SYS to display yellow text on a green display.
see also
DEVICE DRIVER

answering machine
application software that runs on a PC and controls a modem that has voice-mail functionality; using this software your PC can record voice messages or present a caller with a choice of options to record a message, send a fax or connect to a different user
see also
TELEPHONY, VOICE-MAIL

anti-aliasing
technique used to reduce the 'jags' that appear when circles or curves are displayed or printed out. The jags are the steps in the pixels; anti-aliasing fills these gaps with a shade of the colour so that the eye blends these together to give the impression of a smooth curve.

anti-virus software
special software that will hunt out any viruses on your PC and destroy them. MS-DOS 6 has a special set of utilities that will keep a look-out for virus attacks: to check your disks, type in the command 'MSAV' at the prompt.
see also
VIRUS

AOL
see
AMERICA ONLINE

Apache™ HTTPD
the most popular Web server software products, available as freeware, that allows you to setup a Web server; the Apache software is very reliable and efficient, but it is not as friendly or simple to set up as other products

API
APPLICATION PROGRAMMING INTERFACE
set of standard and well documented functions that a programmer can use to control software or hardware.

Apple Macintosh™
very popular range of personal computers developed by Apple. Originally, all Macintosh computers used the Motorola 68000 range of processors, but the latest Macintosh, named the PowerPC, uses a newer, more powerful processor. Although a Macintosh uses a different family and make of processor to IBM-compatible PCs, a Macintosh can run Windows software using special utilities or an add-in board. The Macintosh is operated using a mouse to control a graphical user interface in

which a user points and clicks on objects. Compare this with the MS-DOS way in which a user types in commands.

applet
i) (in Windows) term that is used to refer to small utilities within Microsoft Windows - it originally referred to the icons in the Control Panel window, but now means any utility that configures your system. An application, in contrast, is a full program that you might use every day - like a word-processor program.
ii) (on the internet) small applications designed to enhance the functionality of a Web page; for example, if you want to add multimedia effects to your Web page, you cannot carry out these functions with standard HTML commands, so you could write a small ActiveX program, called an applet, that is automatically downloaded by the user's browser and runs on the user's computer
see also
APPLET, JAVA, VBSCRIPT

application program, application software
program that makes the computer do useful work, such as word processing or a spreadsheet. The five most popular application programs are word processing, accounting, database management, spreadsheet analysis and desktop publishing. Many PCs are now sold with free application software included in the price. Sometimes, these can save you money or can be a waste of time! Suites of application software are also popular: Microsoft Works includes wordprocessing, database, spreadsheet and graphic functions but each is limited compared to a single program dedicated to one task.

application programming interface
see
API

Archie
system of servers on the internet that catalogue the public files available on the internet; you can use Archie to find a particular file and then download it using FTP. There are several ways of using Archie to find a file: you can send an electronic mail message to an Archie server, you can telnet to an Archie server and type in your request, or you can use special Archie software on your computer to carry out the request for you. There are many servers on the internet that store the Archie index of files, in the UK you can try 'archie.doc.ic.ac.uk'. For example, to find files that contain spelling checkers, send an email to 'archie@archie.doc.ic.ac.uk' with a message that reads 'prog spell' and you will get a reply within a few minutes with a list of FTP sites that contain matching files. Alternatively, use a telnet program to connect to the 'archie.doc.ic.ac.uk' site and enter the 'prog spell' command manually
see also
FTP

architecture
general design of a processor, piece of software or computer system. Often used to refer to a type of compatible hardware - for example, Intel architecture means that the computer uses an Intel processor

archive
i) to make a backup of important data and store it away from the computer in case of a fire or burglary. Officially, there is a difference between archiving and making

a backup, but it's not often used! With a backup, you still keep and use the original file on your PC; an archive is for files you want to keep, but don't use and so you move the file off your PC and store it on a disk or tape.

ii) collection of information or files that are available on a server and can be accessed by any user via the internet

see also
BACKUP, RESTORE

archive attribute
one of the attributes stored with any file on a PC. The archive attribute is set to '1' whenever the file is changed and so acts as a reminder to the user (or more usually to tell backup software) that a file has changed since the last backup and so needs to be backed-up again. After copying each file, the back-up program then sets the archive attribute to zero so that the file won't be backed-up again unless it is subsequently changed.

see also
ATTRIBUTE, PROPERTIES

argument
file name or options that are typed on the same line but after a command line command; for example, with the line 'DIR LETTER.DOC', the command is DIR and the argument is 'LETTER.DOC'.

array
list or table of data items. Each `element' within the array is identified by a number that is its position in the array. For example, a program might use an array to hold different tax rates. Element 1 might hold the percentage for the first tax band, element 2 for the second tax band, and so on. Arrays are a central feature of programming and most programming systems, including those in database and spreadsheet packages, provide them.

arrow keys
set of four keys on a keyboard that move the cursor or pointer around the screen; the four keys control movement up, down, left and right.

arrow pointer
small arrow on-screen that you can move using the mouse.
The pointer can change shape to show what's happening in
your PC: it shows an egg-timer (if the computer is busy) or
a I-beam (when you are typing in text).

see also
POINTER

article
one message in a newsgroup; if you want to say something that any other user can read, you would 'post' an article to the newsgroup

see also
NEWSGROUP, POST

artifical intelligence
computers that try and emulate human intelligence; for example, there are now computer programs that ask patients questions to try and establish a possible illness before the patient sees the doctor

ASCII
AMERICAN STANDARD CODE FOR INFORMATION INTERCHANGE

numerical code used to represent characters. For example, A is assigned the value 65, B is 66. ASCII is used by almost all computers, software and communications systems, allowing different computers to exchange data. ASCII is, unfotunately, not completely standardised. The first 128 characters are well defined and normally adhered to; these cover letters, numbers and simple controls such as delete. However, the range of characters between 128 and the limit of ASCII, 255, are far from standard. The 128 character codes abover 128 are called the extended character set and can hold graphics, foreign characters and symbols.

ASIC
APPLICATION SPECIFIC INTEGRATED CIRCUIT

chip that has been specially designed and programmed for a particular function

assembly language, assembler

programming language that uses mnemonics (instructions similar to English-like words) to represent machine code instructions that directly control the processor. An assembly language program is translated into its final numerical form by a program called an assembler. The two terms are often interchanged: people say that a program is written in assembler rather than in assembly language. Assembly language programs are difficult to write and modify. Each instruction does a simple thing (such as move an item of data from memory into the processor) so many thousands are required to create a program that performs a useful job. In contrast, a language like C is `high-level`; particular instructions do more complete tasks, such as printing information or writing it to a file. To use such a language, each high-level instruction is translated by a compiler to a whole sequence of machine code instructions. However, assembly language is the most efficient way to program because it allows the programmer to specify exactly what needs to be done and how, resulting in the smallest and fastest programs. Few applications today are written in assembly language but it is still widely used for system-level software such as device drivers and for parts of large programs that need to run quickly.

asterisk (*)

symbol used to indicate a wildcard in a selection process; if you want to search for all words beginning with 'comp' you could enter 'comp*' and the search will find 'computer', 'computing', 'compatible'; an asterisk translates to mean any number of any characters, unlike a question mark (?) which means any single character

see also
WILDCARD

asynchronous

communication between two devices or operation that does not require a clock signal to time the signals; some communications between two devices send data signals in time with each clock signal (this is called synchronous), asynchronous transfers occur when the devices and data are ready and not regulated by a clock signal

asynchronous cache

type of cache memory that provides the slowest performance and uses a type of SDRAM that is cheap but slow

see also
CACHE, SDRAM

asynchronous transfer mode
see
ATM

asynchronous transmission
common method of transmission between computer and modem, in which each character transmitted is a self-contained unit with its own start and stop bits at irregular intervals; the alternative is synchronous transmission in which both the sending and receiving computers use the same clock signal and so the data does not need to have start or stop bits

AT
PC standard originally developed by IBM that uses a 16-bit 80286 processor. The AT originally meant IBM's Advanced Technology personal computer, but is now used to describe any IBM PC compatible that uses a 16-bit or 32-bit processor (which includes the 80286, 80386 and 80486).

AT-bus
expansion bus standard that was developed by IBM to allow adapter cards to be plugged into the computer. The AT-bus uses a long edge connector inside the computer to carry 16-bits of data and address information between the computer and the adapter card.

AT command set
set of commands that are used to control a modem, developed by Hayes Corporation. All the commands start with the two letters 'AT', for example, ATD123 means dial the number 123. Common commands are ATZ to reset the modem, ATDT123 to dial the number 123 using tone dialing
see also
MODEM, HAYES MODEM

AT-keyboard
standard keyboard layout for an IBM AT personal computer; the keyboard has 102 keys with a row of 12 function keys along the top, compare this with the older XT-keyboard which has the same layout of character keys, but has only 10 function keys arranged to the left of the keyboard.

ATAPI
ADVANCED TECHNOLOGY ATTACHMENT PACKET INTERFACE
a type of standard interface that is used for CD-ROMs

ATM
ASYNCHRONOUS TRANSFER MODE
high speed data transmission system that is often used to link together ISPs or to link servers located at different offices in a company; this technology is gaining in popularity against a fibre-optic link

attachment
file that is transferred together with an electronic mail message. For example, you might have a spreadsheet file called 'ACCOUNTS.XLS' that you include as an attachment with your electronic mail message to your boss. If you have Microsoft Windows for Workgroups, then this includes an electronic mail package, called MS-Mail, which can support the use of attachments. Attachments over the internet

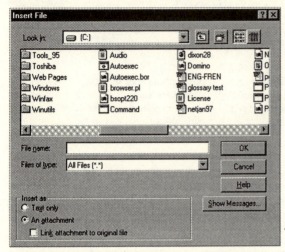

selecting an attachment

are normally sent using the MIME encoding system, but this process is carried out automatically by the electronic mail software

attribute

i) DOS stores a set of six attributes for every file. These settings can either be on or off and are recorded in the directory entry for the file that reflects some aspect of its status. For example, each file has a 'Read-only' attribute. If this is 'on' (also called 'set'), DOS will not allow the file to be altered, updated or deleted. If it is off (also called 'reset' or 'clear') then the file may be updated. The attributes read-only, archive, hidden and system may be altered by users using software such as the DOS ATTRIB command. The other two attributes, Volume and Directory, are used internally by DOS to identify volume label and sub-directory entries, as opposed to files, within a directory.

ii) Programming term for the colour intensity or style in which a character is displayed or printed.

audio

sound; for a computer to produce sound, it needs a sound card that fits inside the computer together with speakers. The sound card converts digital information from the computer into analog sound signals that are then amplified and played through speakers

see also

ANALOG

audio file

file that contains digital sample data from a sound. In Windows, audio files normally have a WAV extension and are played back or recorded using the Sound Recorder utility in the Accessories group.

audio/video interleaved (AVI)

Standard, devised by Microsoft, that describes how video frames and simultaneous sound should be stored in a single file. In a PC, these files have an AVI extension and can be played back using the MediaPlayer utility in the Accessories group.

AUI
ATTACHMENT UNIT INTERFACE
connector used to connect a network cable to some types of Ethernet network card

AUP
ACCEPTABLE USE POLICY
set of rules that describe what a user can write or do on the internet without offending other users; many ISPs publish their own set of AUP rules for their customers

authoring
Creating a multimedia book using special software or creating a WWW page using HTML codes to format images and text

authoring software
Special application that allows you to create multimedia programs. Authoring software lets you design the pages of the multimedia book, and place video clips, images, text and sound on a page. Almost all multimedia developers use some type of authoring software rather than a traditional programming language because it is a much faster and easier way to create multimedia programs.

AUTOEXEC.BAT
One of two special text files that the user can create to control the startup process of a PC. AUTOEXEC.BAT is a batch file placed in the root directory of the disk used to start the PC (usually the hard disk if one is fitted or a floppy in drive A:). If this file is present, it is automatically executed once DOS is loaded (hence the name). The other startup file is CONFIG.SYS which contains special instructions rather than ordinary DOS commands that set up DOS initially. If your PC is already set up, you probably already have an AUTOEXEC.BAT file on your startup disk(s). You can check this with a command such as DIR C:\AUTOEXEC.BAT (hard disk) or DIR A:\AUTOEXEC.BAT (floppy system). Use TYPE rather than DIR to list what is in the file. You should be careful not to delete an existing AUTOEXEC.BAT file or to make inappropriate changes to it as it may prevent software and add-ons from working properly.

It is not necessary to have an AUTOEXEC.BAT file. Without one, DOS will ask for the time and date when it starts and then display the DOS prompt ready for commands. As most PCs now have a battery clock and calendar, you can disable these prompts by creating an AUTOEXEC.BAT file even if it contains no commands at all.

AUTOEXEC.BAT is a plain text file listing DOS commands (or commands to start programs) one per line. You can create a short one using the COPY command but it is better to use a text editor or word processor (see creating and editing text files). It's entirely up to you what commands should be placed in AUTOEXEC.BAT. Certain commands may be necessary for your software, such as SET, or to load special TSR programs. Almost all AUTOEXEC.BAT files on a hard disk contain a PATH command to tell DOS which directories to look in for program files and a KEYB or command to setup the keyboard layout. Many finish with a command to go straight into a particular package or start a menu program running rather than presenting the DOS prompt.

It is a good idea to create a back-up of your AUTOEXEC.BAT file by copying it to another disk and to make a printed listing of it. This will allow the file to be restored should it be necessary. A common trap is that some software packages make their own alterations to AUTOEXEC.BAT when first installed on a system and these are not always suitable and may prevent other programs from operating. Demanding users may find that they need different AUTOEXEC.BAT (and CONFIG.SYS) files at different times. Rather than continually altering the existing file, you can use COPY to create several different versions under different names, such as AUTOEXEC.WIN for a Windows-related AUTOEXEC.BAT. These can then be quickly copied over the current AUTOEXEC.BAT file to select them. Utility programs which automate this process are available. Finally, remember that AUTOEXEC.BAT is carried out once when the PC starts so any alterations to it do not take affect until the PC is next restarted (e.g. by pressing [Ctrl]-[Alt]-[Del]). You can of course run AUTOEXEC.BAT by entering the command AUTOEXEC but if it loads any TSR type programs these may be inadvertently loaded a second time. If your AUTOEXEC.BAT (or CONFIG.SYS) file has a problem which prevents the PC from starting, use an original DOS startup disk to get to the DOS prompt and then amend the files as necessary. In the case of AUTOEXEC.BAT, it's possible to cancel execution by pressing [Ctrl]-[Break] as DOS starts to process the file but this can be hit and miss.

see also
CONFIG.SYS

automatic mailing list

see
LISTSERV

autosync

feature of a modem that allows it to transfer synchronous data signals to and from a computer that can only transfer asynchronous signals; if you want to connect your personal computer to a synchronous data source (such as a mainframe computer) you would need to install a special adapter card or use a modem that can convert the asynchronous data from your computer's serial port to synchronous data

AVI

file format used to store video clips and audio sections

Bb

BABT approval

official approval required before a new modem can be sold and be connected to the UK telephone network; the approval does not provide any quality assurance about the modem, but ensures that it is manufactured in such a way that it does not damage the telephone network. A green label is visible on modem equipment that has received BABT approval

back door

unauthorised route into a computer system that by-passes the main security or password protection scheme

backbone

very fast communications link that connects major ISPs together across the world. Large companies may also have a high-speed backbone linking many network servers together.

see also

T1

background

i) a picture that is displayed behind the main windows and icons on your desktop. In Windows you can define the colour and pattern of the background (which is also called wallpaper), or you can display an image.

ii) something that's happening automatically, whilst you are working on something different.

background printing

method of sending information from your PC to the printer whilst you are running some other application. For example, Windows uses a utility called Print Manager to temporarily store any document that you print; it then prints out the documents whilst you can carry on working on another document. Without background printing (that's also sometimes called spooling or print queuing), you would not be able to use your word processor until it had finished printing out all the pages of your document - which could be a long time if you have a slow printer.

backlit display

(in a laptop computer) very thin light that is behind the display and shines through, improving the contrast and visibility of the characters and images on the display. This is part of most monochrome LCD displays used in laptops. Newer colour displays use a different method of producing a very bright, clear image. A monitor on your desk works like a television and uses an electron beam to illuminate tiny dots of phosphor that coat the inside of the glass screen.

backup

second, safe copy of a file, letter or data. You should always do regular backups of your important work: it might seem very boring at the time, but it's far more boring to type all the information back in again! You normally backup your data onto a little cassette tape or, if you don't have too much, onto floppy disks. Windows includes a utility that will make backing up painless: just tell it which folder, directory or file you want to copy and whether you want to make a backup onto a floppy disk or tape and it does all the copying. Once you have made a backup, keep it well away from your main computer: if there's a fire then both your PC and the backup will be destroyed. Ensure that you make a new backup of the latest versions of your data at least once a week. If you ever need to access the files you've backed up, you need to use another utility that will restore them. This copies them from the floppy disk or tape back to the correct folder or directory.

compare with
RESTORE

backup agent

Windows 95 includes software utilities that will carry out an automatic backup of a set of files or folders for you at a regular time and date each week. Click on Start/Programs/Applications and you'll see the backup agent.

backwards compatible

new computer that will work with all the old adapter cards designed for earlier versions of the computer, or a new piece of software that provides the same functions as the previous version and can read the files created in the previous version. For example, Windows 95 is backwards compatible with Windows 3.x since it can run the same programs. Microsoft Word 6 is backwards compatible with Word 2, and provides the original functions (plus new ones) and can read documents written with Word 2.

bad sector

fault with a floppy disk or hard disk. Disks are divided up into tracks which contain many sectors; each sector can hold hundreds of bytes (often 256 or 512 bytes of data). If you have a bad sector, it means that the disk surface has been damaged at this point and that the disk drive cannot read the data that was stored there. In short, you will either have a corrupted file or will not be able to read the file. To fix it, use the disk tools in Windows 95 or run Scandisk from the MS-DOS prompt. For serious faults, use a special program like Norton's Disk Doctor or Symantec PC Tools to try and fix the sector.

bandwidth

measure of the amount of data that can be transferred over a link or circuit; for example, the bandwidth of an Ethernet network is normally 10Mbps, but this is normally only reached if a lot of users are transferring data over the network at the same time

bank

row or group of components that make up a single device; for example, if you increase the memory in your computer you might fit more memory chips to the existing bank (or collection) of memory chips

bank switching

method of managing a group of memory components so that they appear like pages in a book; each page can contain data. This scheme was used in PC computers

running DOS; the DOS operating system could only handle limited memory capacity and this scheme proved a way of expanding the amount of usable memory
see also
VIRTUAL MEMORY

banner
message or advertisement or image that is displayed on a Web page; there is now an unofficial standard size for banner advertisements that is a long, narrow strip

banner page
page that is printed out first with the time, date, name of the document and the name of the person who has printed it. If you are working by yourself, you can turn this feature off from within Windows (use the Control Panel/Printers icon) or you will waste lots of paper.

bar chart
graph on which values are displayed as vertical or horizontal bars.

bar
see
TOOLBAR

base font
font and point size used by a wordprocessing package or DTP package if no style has been selected. This is normally a Times font that is displayed in 10point.

base hardware
minimum specifications for a PC that can run a particular software package. These are normally printed on the side of the software package. For example, if you want to run Windows you will need a PC with 4Mb of RAM fitted, at least 20Mb of free hard disk space and an 80386 or better processor. Graphics programs often demand more sophisticated base hardware with more memory or a faster processor.

base memory or conventional memory
(in an IBM-compatible PC) the term that describes the first 640Kb of memory installed. Due to a historical design 'feature', MS-DOS and other software handles the first 640Kb of memory in a different way to the rest of the memory that's installed. If your PC has 4Mb of RAM fitted, the first 640Kb is called the base or conventional memory, the next 384Kb is called the upper memory and the remaining 3Mb is called extended memory.
see also
EXTENDED MEMORY, UPPER MEMORY

BASIC
BEGINNER'S ALL-PURPOSE SYMBOLIC INSTRUCTION CODE
programming language that uses instructions that sound like English words. MS-DOS comes with a copy of BASIC, called QBASIC, that lets you experiment with programming. Each line of the program is numbered and the lines contain program instructions that can calculate, open files, draw images, or print. Microsoft has a sophisticated version of Basic, called Visual Basic, that allows users to easily create Windows programs with little knowledge of programming

BAT
three letter file name extension that's given to batch program files that contain batch

commands stored as text

batch file

text file stored on disk that contains MS-DOS commands that you can type at the MS-DOS command prompt, together with some other special control commands. It's a convenient way of grouping together a series of commands that you need to run frequently. To run all the commands stored in the batch file, just type in the name of the batch file (without its BAT extension) and each line will be run consecutively. When you first switch on your PC a batch file called AUTOEXEC.BAT is run automatically. This contains all the setup and configuration commands that define the environment and setup any special devices - like a CD-ROM drive or network. To see if you have any batch files on your hard disk, use the 'DIR *.BAT' command from the MS-DOS prompt or the File Manager/Explorer in Windows and look for the BAT file extension. To see what's inside a batch file, use the TYPE command in MS-DOS or open the batch file using a word processor or Notebook or WordPad.

battery meter

(in a laptop computer) utility that tells you how much life or working time you have left in your batteries. In Windows 95, a tiny icon appears in the bottom right-hand corner of the screen and this shows you when you are about to run out of battery power and need to recharge.

baud or baud rate

measure of the number of signal changes that occur in a signal every second. Modems and many other communications devices are sometimes described in terms of a baud rate. It's important to note that baud is not the same as the amount of data sent every second - see bits per second; with clever compression techniques, it's possible to send more data than there are signal changes.

bay

space within a computer's case into which you can fit and secure a floppy disk drive or CD-ROM drive or hard disk drive. If you look at the front of your PC, you'll notice a floppy disk drive and, if you have one, a CD-ROM drive. If there's a blank plate below one of these drives then behind this is an empty bay into which you could fit another drive. To fit the drive into the bay you must open the case and connect the drive to the correct controller card.

BBS

BULLETIN BOARD SYSTEM

computer that supports remote users who connect via a modem link and can read and send messages and download files; bulletin board systems used to be very popular with hobby groups but were not interconnected. The internet replaced most bulletin board systems as the standard way of exchanging information between groups of people

bcc

see

BLIND CARBON COPY

benchmark

program that measures the speed of the different components in your PC to get an overall impression of how fast and powerful your computer configuration is compared with another computer.

beta software
early version of a software product that is still being tested and is not yet working properly, or still has a few bugs. Avoid using beta software for regular use, since it's not completely reliable. When all the bugs have been found and fixed, the software is then released.

Bézier curve
geometric curve in which the overall shape is defined by two endpoints, called control handles. Bézier curves are a feature of many high-end design software packages sice they allow the designer to draw complex, but smooth curves.

binary
common name for base 2 arithmetic. In binary, the smallest unit is a bit (short for a binary digit) and this can have one of just two values: zero or one. Computers do all their calculations using binary arithmetic, since the two values are easy to represent electrically: as zero volts for zero and (normally) five volts for a one. By comparison, in base ten (decimal) each digit can have one of ten (zero to nine) values.

binary file
file that contains non-text information, such as a graphic image or a program file; if you want to send a binary file via electronic mail to another user, you need to send it as a MIME attachment, or encode it using uuencode
see
MIME, UUENCODE

BIOS
BASIC INPUT/OUTPUT SYSTEM
series of instructions that manage the basic functions within your computer. For example, the BIOS looks after how the keyboard works and makes sure that the right character code is sent when you press a key. It also manages the disk drives and the monitor. A software application, like a word processing program, carries out tasks by asking the BIOS to do the real work. It asks the BIOS if the user has typed any text; if they have, it asks the BIOS to display the character. You don't have to worry about the BIOS, and you are very unlikely to ever see it, since it's stored on a chip inside your computer. However, it's responsible for the real work and you'll see a message displaying the version number, date and company that developed the BIOS software routines appear when you switch on your PC.

bit
smallest unit in the binary or base two arithmetic system. Bit is short for a binary digit, and a bit can have one of just two values: zero or one. Data is stored in a computer as a combination of bits (eight together are referred to as a byte)
see also
BINARY

bit block transfer or bitBLT
process of moving the contents of a section of memory from one location to another; usually used to update a screen image or during animation

bitFTP
type of server that allows a user to retrieve a file using only an email link; the user

sends an email to the bitFTP server, the email contains a series of FTP commands that ask it to fetch the file from a remote server, when it has done this, the bitFTP server sends an email back to the user as an email attachment or encoded mail message. If you want to retrieve a file, send a message that contains just 'help' to 'ftpmail@doc.ic.ac.uk' to find out how the system works

bitmap

image that is made up of thousands of tiny dots (or pixels); the colour of each dot is controlled by the value stored in the bitmap file for that position. If you zoom in on a bitmap image you will see the dots grow larger and larger. Compare this with a vector image, in which the shapes are described mathematically and so they appear sharp however much you zoom in on the image. If you look at Windows, every icon picture is stored as a small bitmap image. You can paint your own bitmap images by using the Paint utility in the Accessories folder. When you paint an image, you are colouring in the dots - to see what each dot looks like in close up, use the zoom function.

bitmapped font

type of font in which the shape of each character is defined by a pattern of dots in a matrix. Bitmapped fonts are quick and easy for a computer or printer to use, but they are of a fixed size: if you try and increase the size, you will see all the dots enlarged and the characters will appear very jagged. To counter this, outline fonts were developed: TrueType fonts or ATM fonts or PostScript fonts are used by Windows; these describe each character shape as a series of curves and matematical equations. It means that you can change the size of the character and it will always have a smooth outline.

compare with

OUTLINE FONT

BitNet

network used to connect (mostly) academic sites and computers and allows transfer of electronic mail and listserver application; BitNet is similar to the internet and is connected to allow the transfer of electronic mail to and from academic users to other users on the internet

bits per second (bps)

way of describing the speed of a modem or serial link between two computers or a computer and a printer. It means how many single bits of data can be sent by the computer every second. If you are checking the specification of a modem, make sure that it is describing bits per second and not baud rate. For example, a fast modem that can support 14,400bits per second will probably use a slower baud rate because it includes some clever electronics. By compressing the data before it is sent, modems can easily send 30,000 bits every second. If you want to think of how many characters of text this means, divide the number by eight to get the number of bytes (or characters) transmitted every second. For modems, the standard transmission speed is now 28,800bps, 33,600bps is fast and the newest is 56,600bps. If you link two computers together with a serial cable you can transfer files between the two (useful when transferring files between a laptop and a desk PC). Windows 95 includes a utility that called direct-cable transfer that lets you send files between two computers at high speeds: the maximum is normally 115,200bps.

BIX

commercial online system founded by Byte magazine; contains a lot of technical and programming topics

biz

type of newsgroup that contains business discussions and oportunities; for example, 'biz.oportunities' contains messages from users that are offering ways of making money. Only the biz series of newsgroups are supposed to discuss commercial aspects, the rest of the newsgroups are for technical or academic discussion
compare with
ALT

blind carbon copy (bcc)

feature of many electronic mail programs that allows a user to send one message to several users at a time (carbon copy) but does not display this list to the recipients

blink

way a cursor flashes on and off to show you where you are positioned on the screen or in a document.

block

section of text that you have marked before moving, deleting or editing it. If you use a Windows wordprocessing program, you can mark a block of text by moving to cursor to the start and clicking and holding down the left-hand mouse button then, with the button held down, move to the end of the section of text. You'll see the block highlighted in reverse. Once you have selected the block, let go of the mouse button; you can now delete the block or change its fonts or size, or move it using cut and paste from the Edit menu.

BMP

three letter file name extension that's given to files that store bitmap image data. If you use the Paint utility in Windows, you can save or open BMP files created in any other paint program; you can also insert BMP files into some wordprocessing packages to enhance your letters or reports.
see also
GIF, JPEG, TIFF

body or body text

i) main text of a document or book. If you use a Windows wordprocessing package that lets you define styles, there is probably a default style for the body text that is used if no other is specified.
ii):main part of an electronic mail message
compare with
HEADER, ATTACHMENT

bomb

(software or computer system) to fail or not work correctly

book

multimedia title. The name comes from the fact that most multimedia titles are arranged as a series of different pages which together form a book.

bookmark

code used by a multimedia title or wordprocessor or Web browser that allows the user to move straight back to this point at a later date. The software keeps a list of all the bookmarks you have inserted together with the relevant page number.

Boolean

mathematical functions that refer to binary logical operations that define the way in which a computer works. If you search for text in a multimedia encyclopaedia or on the internet, you will probably use Boolean operators: AND, OR, XOR, NOT. For example, searching for 'cat AND dog' will find any entry that contains the word 'cat' and the word 'dog'. In binary (base two) arithmetic, Boolean operators work in a similar way: 1 AND 1 is equal to 1; 1 AND 0 is equal to 0; 1 OR 1 is equal to 1; 1 OR 0 is equal to 1.

Boolean search

search that uses the AND and OR functions

bootable

storage device that holds the commands to boot up a computer and load the operating system; your main hard disk is a bootable device and your computer will normally boot up from this disk unless you insert a floppy disk into drive A: (in which case the computer looks on drive A: for the operating system)

boot disk

disk that contains the operating system that is loaded when a PC is switched on. The boot up instructions tell the hardware to read in the operating system software. Normally, the boot disk is your main hard disk. However, you can use a floppy disk as a boot disk, if it is formatted as a system or boot disk (using the Format /S command).

boot sector

part of a disk that contains instructions that are read by the computer when it is first switched on or reset; the instructions tell the computer how to load the operating system from the disk

boot up

process that is carried out when your PC is switched on. First, a sequence of instructions stored with the BIOS in a chip are executed and these tell the computer to look on the boot disk for the main operating system. The PC tests the floppy drive A: and the then the hard drive C: for a valid boot disk that contains the operating system.

border

thin line around a window or box or button or image. If you are using a DTP application, the border style command will change the look of the lines around a box or image. For example, you could change the border to show a double line or a dashed line border style.

bounce

electronic mail that is returned to the sender because the address is incorrect or the user is not known at the mail server

bounding box

rectangle that determines the shape and position of an image that's been placed in a document or on screen. In graphics applications there is normally a special tool that allows you to select an area of an image to operate on: this area is shown as a dashed or flashing bounding box and can be stretched by moving the mouse.

bps
BITS PER SECOND

measure of data communications speed. Often confused with baud, which refers to the number of transitions made per second and which equals bps only at low speeds, such as 300 bps.

break
to stop or interrupt a program; on a PC there are two ways to stop or interrupt a program, either by pressing the Esc key (in the top left-hand corner) which normally interrupts a process such as a search and replace in a wordprocessor; if this does not work, pressing Ctrl-C will also sometimes work or, lastly, pressing Ctrl-Break will also sometimes interrupt a program that is not working correctly

bridge
interconnection device that can connect LANs at the data link level so allowing similar LANs using different transmission methods, for example Ethernet or Token Ring, to transfer information. Bridges are able to read and filter the data packets and frames employed by the protocol and use the addresses to decide whether or not to pass a packet.

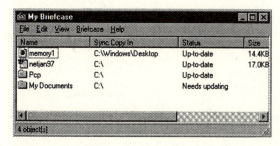

Briefcase utility

Briefcase utility
(in Windows 95) a special utility that allows you to keep files stored on a laptop and a desktop PC up to date. The briefcase utility is just like a real briefcase: you insert files or folder into the electronic briefcase and Windows will ensure that the files are kept up to date. It is very useful if you travel away from the office and need to work on some documents or files on a laptop; when you get back to the office you can connect the laptop to your main desktop PC and the Briefcase utility will update the files on each computer. In order to use the Briefcase utility you will need a serial cable to connect the two computers and you will have to install the option from the Windows/Control Panel/Install Programs option.

brouter
device that combines the functions of a bridge and router in connecting two networks. A brouter will route data packets if the protocol is known and bridge them if the protocol is unknown.

browser
software program that is used to navigate through WWW pages stored on the internet; a browser program asks the internet server (called the HTTP server) to send it a page of information, this page is stored in the HTML layout language that

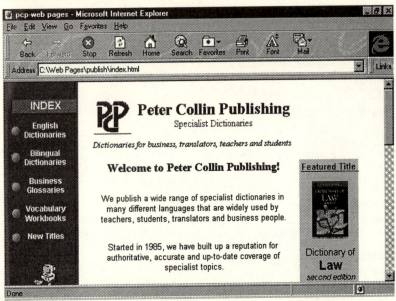

Microsoft Internet Explorer web browser

is decoded by the browser and displayed on screen. The browser displays any hotspots and hyperlinks and will jump to another page if you click on a hyperlink.

see also
HTML, NETSCAPE, INTERNET EXPLORER

browsing

to move through a multimedia title or through a list of files or through sites on the internet in no particular order. You control which page you move to next and what you view.

brush

tool in a paint program that lets you draw a line on the screen. You can normally change the colour of the paint on the brush, together with the width of the brush. In the Paint program in Windows, the colour used and the width of the brush are defined in the bottom left-hand corner. If you draw a line it will appear as if it has been painted with the brush, in the colour and width of the brush.

bubble-help

single line that appears on screen to describe what you are pointing at: if you're not sure what a button does, move the pointer over it and wait a second or two and a little one-line description will pop-up (not all software has bubble help)

buffer

area of memory that is used for temporary storage of information before it's needed. If you type very fast, the wordprocessor software might not be able to display the characters as quickly as you type them in, so the keystrokes are stored in a keyboard buffer. Similarly, if you print a document before you have switched the printer on, the data is stored in a print buffer until the printer has been switched on and ready to print.

bug

error in a computer program that means it does not work properly.
See also
BETA

built-in

feature that is already included in a computer. For example, it's normal for computers to have a hard disk and a floppy disk drive built-in as standard.

bullet

symbol (often a filled circle or square) printed or displayed in front of a line of text and used to draw attention to the text. If you are creating a presentation, you can indicate and highlight the important points of the meeting by placing a bullet symbol in front of each point. If you are using a Windows wordprocessor, you can add a bullet by changing the font to Symbol or Wingdings and choosing one of the many bullet characters - to see all the characters in a font, use the Character Map utility in Windows and cut-and-paste the character into your document.

bulletin board (BBS)

computer that you can call up and connect to via a modem and a telephone line. Bulletin boards normally have lots of free software that you can download onto your computer, together with forums where you can discuss topics with other users. Most BBSs have electronic mail facilities that lets you send messages to other users. More sophisticated BBS systems have links to other BBS computers or even the internet, so that you can send and receive messages to a user on another system. When you first sign-up with a bulletin board you are given an account which has your own user name and a password. To use the BBS again, you need to enter your user name and password. Some BBS computers limit the amount of time for which you can use the system, or limit the number of files that you can download. Normally a bulletin board is run either as a hobby by a keen computer-lover or by a school or university. The person in charge of the bulletin board is called the SYSOP (system operator). Bulletin boards are rarely professional - except for some computer companies that use a bulletin board to provide support for their products. Systems that are run on a professional basis tend to be called on-line services (it sounds more professional!). These normally charge you to connect to the computer but provide a lot more business-oriented information, like share prices. To access a bulletin board you need to have a modem connected to your computer. This will convert the data from the computer into sounds that it can then send along a normal phone line to the BBS computer. You also need communications software that will dial up the BBS and manage the modem. All versions of Windows come with free communications software to get you started: in Windows 3.x this is called Terminal in the Accessories group, in Windows 95 it's called HyperTerminal and needs to be installed separately as an option. Some professional on-line services, like CompuServe, have their own customised communications software.

bundle

special deal available when buying a computer system or software package that includes extras that would normally cost more to buy separately. For example, if you are lucky, you might find a shop that has a special offer: buy a computer and printer and get free paper. Software bundles can sometimes mean an application that will carry out all the functions a user might want for everyday use. For example, Microsoft Works is a software bundle (that is often included as a bundle deal when you buy a PC) and includes a simple wordprocessor, database, spreadsheet, and graphics program.

bureau
company that specializes in printing out high-quality images or typesetting text prepared using a desktop publishing program. A bureau normally has a typesetting machine that can produce very high quality text or black and white images onto film or photographic paper ready for a professional printer. Bureaux can also scan in colour photographs or slides at a very high resolution.

burst mode
method of transmitting data in a computer in which a particular device in the computer (such as the memory controller, graphics adapter or disk controller) will take control of the main data bus and transmit a lot of data to another device all in one go rather than waiting for the central processor to allow it to transmit data in several short sessions

bus
set of wires or cables that connect the main parts of the computer together. For example, the data bus is normally made up of 16 wires and carries the data around the computer, from the processor to the memory or hard disk controller. In practice, the wires are actually thin copper lines on the motherboard inside your computer. There are usually three main buses within a computer: address bus, data bus and control bus. The address bus carries the memory location for the data that's travelling at the same time on the data bus. The third is the control bus, and this carries a whole set of control and timing signals to make sure that all the components are working together.

bus clock speed
frequency of the clock that governs the main bus in a computer, which is not necessarily the same frequency as the clock speed of the main central processor
see also
WAIT STATE

bus master
device in your PC that is able to control the bus. Normally, this would be the processor, but in high-performance computers, the video adapter or disk controller can take over control of the bus to allow it to exchange data very rapidly with the main memory. In short, it's a way of moving data to and from main memory without troubling the processor. If your PC has a bus master graphics card it can transfer data and draw images on screen faster than a normal graphics card.
see also
LOCAL BUS

bus topology
way of designing a network in which all the connections are linked as branches to one central main cable. This is the usual topology for networks based on an Ethernet transmission system, wheras Token Ring and 10Base-T both use a ring topology. Bus networks are easy to implement, but one break in the wire brings the whole network down. Star topology networks (such as 10Base-T) avoid this problem using one central connection point - the hub - with lots of short wires to each node

button
square shape that's displayed on the screen. When you move the pointer over the

button and click on the mouse button, something will happen. For example, when you want to leave Windows it displays a small box with the message 'are you sure you want to leave' and two buttons labelled 'OK' and 'Cancel'. If you move the pointer over the OK button and click on the mouse button, you'll quit Windows. Similarly, in Windows 95 there's always a Start button displayed in the bottom left-hand corner of the screen: move over this and click and you'll see a menu of options. Just to confuse the issue, there are all sorts of buttons, but radio buttons and push-buttons are the most common. A radio button lets you choose only one from a number of possible options (unlike a check-box), whilst a push-button starts some action. In many multimedia applications, or in a WWW page on the internet, you'll see images that are used as buttons, or areas of the screen that start an action if you click on them. These are normally called hot-spots to differentiate between this special type of button and a normal visible button.

button bar

line of tiny buttons along the top of the screen - just below the menu bar - in many applications such as Microsoft Word, Works and Excel. Each button on the bar contains a picture (called an icon) that helps describe the function of the button. If you're not sure what the picture means then move the pointer over the button and wait for a few seconds without clicking: in many applications you should see a description of the button pop up beside it.

byte

group of eight bits (that's eight binary digits) which is the usual form in which data is manipulated within a computer. One byte can hold numbers between zero and 255. For example, each different character in the alphabet has a special code that describes it (see ASCII code). This code is stored within one byte, and so your computer can identify 256 different characters.

see also

BINARY, BIT, WORD

Cc

C

programming language that is usually used by professional programmers to create applications; C is more complex than BASIC but produces applications that run much faster and more efficiently

C++

programming language that is usually used by professional programmers to create applications. C++ is derived from the C programming language and is often considered better for Windows programming since it allows programmers to create object-oriented applications

C: drive

letter that is used in some operating systems, including DOS, Windows and OS/2 and that denotes the hard disk drive on the system. Normally, a PC has two or three disk drives within its casing. One floppy disk, called 'A:' and one hard disk called 'C:'. If you have a second floppy disk, this is called 'B:' and a CD-ROM drive is normally 'D:'. When talking about the different disk drives, you say 'Drive C' for the hard disk, but normally write 'C:'. If you are using DOS, when your PC starts up it will normally show what's called the C-prompt (which looks like 'C:\>' on your screen); this means you are currently looking at the hard disk.

see also
FLOPPY DISK, HARD DISK

cable

collection of wires
see also
DIRECT CABLE, NULL MODEM CABLE, PRINTER CABLE, RIBBON CABLE

cache

(electronic memory components that provide) section of very high-speed memory that is used to temporarily store data before it is used by the computer's processor. A cache can dramatically speed up the effective rate at which data is read from a hard disk drive: the computer reads more data than is requested and stores the excess in the cache ready to be accessed with the next request to read data. The memory used for the cache can be up to 100,000 times faster than a hard disk drive

CAD

COMPUTER AIDED-DESIGN
software application that allows designers and architects to draw precise blueprints on screen, then model them in three dimensions to see how the design will appear in real life before it is manufactured.

caddy
see
CD CADDY

Calculator
software utility that's supplied with Windows and works just like a normal
calculator. To start the Calculator, double-click on the icon in the Accessories group
of Windows 3.1 or choose Start/Programs/Accessories in Windows 95.

Calendar™
simple calendar and diary that was supplied with Windows 3.1. This has been
replaced by the more sophisticated Schedule+ in Windows 3.11 and Windows 95.

calibrate
to adjust a monitor or joystick so that is is responding correctly and accurately to
the signals or movements. For example, this ensures that the monitor is displaying a
true representation of the colour that will be printed.

callback
security system that's used to reduce the risk of any unauthorised user connecting to
your computer if you have installed dial-in networking (part of Windows 95).
Callback works in a simple but effective way: you use your communications
software and modem to dial the remote computer and enter your name and
password. The remote computer then hangs up the telephone line and calls you back
on a preset telephone number.

call discrimination
feature of a modem that allows it to check if an incoming telephone call is from a
fax machine, another computer with a modem or from a person; this feature is
useful if you have one telephone line and are using your modem to receive fax
transmissions and spoken messages

Cancel
button that is normally displayed beside an OK button to give you a chance to stop
the action you were about to carry out

Caps Lock key
key on a PC keyboard (on the left-hand side) that switches the letters typed between
lowercase and uppercase; this key works as a toggle - press once to switch to
uppercase, press again to switch to lowercase

caption
descriptive text that appears at the top of a window, in white text on a blue
background: for example, in Windows 95, double-click on the MyComputer icon
and you'll see a small window pop up; the top of the window has the caption: My
Computer in white characters on a blue background. If you click anywhere outside
this window, the blue background to the caption turns grey, to show that the
window is no longer active (see active window).

capture (a printer port)
way of redirecting data intended for a printer port over a network to a shared
printer; when several PCs are connected together to form a workgroup or network,
one computer will be connected to a shared printer. To use this shared printer, you
have to tell Windows that you want anything that's normally sent to the printer port

on your computer redirected over the network to the shared printer: this can be setup using the Printer icon in the Control Panel group.

capture (a screen)

to store the image that is currently displayed on the screen in a file. In Windows, you can save the current screen as a graphics image by pressing the PrintScreen key on the keyboard; this graphics image can then be pasted into a document or paint program (start the Windows Paint program and choose the Edit/Paste menu command to paste the image of the screen).

carbon copy (cc)

feature of electronic mail software that allows you to send a copy of a message to another user

see also
BLIND CARBON COPY

card

i) see adapter card; ii) a single page in a multimedia book; if you have bought a multimedia application about dinosaurs (called the multimedia book), each dinosaur is described on a page or card which might contain pictures, sound, text, and buttons.

caret (^)

i) symbol that is normally used in manuals to represent the Ctrl key, for example ^C means hold down the Ctrl key and press the C key at the same time; ii) means 'raise to a power of', for example 2^4 means 2 raised to the power of 4.

carriage return (CR)

historically, this is a printer command that moves the print head (before the days of laser printers) to the start of a line; now it tends to mean the same as the Return key

see
RETURN KEY

carrier (signal)

continuous, steady sound tone that is used by a modem to send data along a telephone wire. The modem changes the frequency of the carrier (the tone) to represent different characters. If you have a modem and connect to an on-line service (such as Microsoft Network, CompuServe or CIX) you can tell when your modem has recognised the distant modem when the carrier detect (CD) light lights up on the front of your modem.

CAS

COMMUNICATING APPLICATIONS SPECIFICATION
standard developed by Intel and DCA for software control for FAX/modems.

cascading windows

way of arranging lots of windows on screen so that they overlap, with only the title bar and caption of each window showing. This is a much neater and more efficient way of displaying lots of windows on the screen at the same time. The alternative is to tile the windows: each is displayed beside the next with no overlap. Another alternative is to minimise each window into an icon (or, in Windows 95, onto the status bar along the bottom of the screen).

case-sensitive

software that can detect the difference between lower-case and upper-case characters; for example, if you have a case-sensitve password then 'Fred' will not be the same as 'fred'. You're more likely to find this as a feature of search and replace functions in a wordprocessor.

cast

each individual part of a multimedia presentation or animation: the members of a cast can be individual images, sound clips or text.

cc

see
CARBON COPY

CCD

CHARGE-COUPLED DEVICE

tiny electronic component that has an array of thousands of light-sensitive cells on its surface; a CCD component is used in video cameras, electronic cameras and some scanners to detect a picture and turn it into electronic signals that can be processed by a computer.

CCITT

COMITÉ CONSULTATIF INTERNATIONALE DE TÉLÉGRAPHIE ET TÉLÉPHONIE

United Nations group responsible for setting international telecommunications standards. Its recommendations for telephone lines always start with the letter V

CD

COMPACT DISC

small plastic disc that is used to store masses of data: up to 650Mb of data. The data is stored in the form of tiny holes etched into the surface of the disc; a CD drive spins the disc and uses a laser beam to read the holes in the surface. A CD can store any type of computer data from images to text to music. However, it can only be read by a user - you cannot save data onto a CD. A CD normally refers to a normal music disc which can be played in your HiFi or in your PC's CD player (just plug in a pair of headphones and use the MediaPlayer utility to start playing). In the computer world, the same type of plastic disc is used to store files and data and is called a CD-ROM (Read Only Memory).

CD caddy

flat plastic container that is used to hold a compact disc. The caddy is inserted into a CD-ROM drive: some CD-ROM drives use a caddy to hold the disc, others use a motorised tray onto which the 'bare' compact disc is place. Remember to place the compact disc with the printed side facing up so that you can see the printed side through the transparent top of the caddy.

CD-audio or CD-DA

COMPACT DISC-DIGITAL AUDIO

standard that defines how music can be stored as a series of numbers (digital form) on a compact disc.

CD-I

COMPACT DISC-INTERACTIVE

set of enhancements to the normal CD-ROM standard, developed by Philips, and aimed for home use. The system uses its own special hardware console with speakers, joystick and a connection to a television screen to display the images. The special feature of CD-I is that it allows you to interact with what you see on the television screen and choose options or respond to questions or a game.

CD-ROM XA

enhanced method of storing data onto a CD-ROM disc that lets the computer read sound from the disc at the same time as images or text. If you want to play a CD-ROM XA disc on your computer, you will need to make sure that the CD-ROM drive is XA compliant. Watch out! Some PC manufacturers get confused between CD-ROM XA and PhotoCD compatible: a CD-ROM XA drive can read a PhotoCD.

CD-ROM

see
CD

CD-ROM drive

mechanical device that spins a compact disc and reads data stored on the surface of the disc using a tiny laser beam

cel

single frame in an animation sequence; computer animations are normally made up of lots of images that are each slightly different. When the sequence of images is displayed one after the other, the action appears to move. Each separate image is a cel.

Cello™

older Web browser application that has been overtaken by Netscape Navigator and Microsoft IE

centre text

option in every wordprocessing package that lets you place the line or paragraph of text in the centre of the page. Move the cursor to the line of text then click the centre text format button or choose Format/Paragraph/Alignment/Centre menu option (in Microsoft Word).

Centronics port

standard that defines the way in which a parallel printer port on a PC operates
see also
PARALLEL PORT

CERN

research laboratory in Switzerland where the world wide web was originally invented

CGA

COLOR GRAPHICS ADAPTER
very early graphics adapter standard developed by IBM; you'll hardly ever see this now except in the setup program for your computer - CGA provides few colours at

a low resoloution and was replaced by EGA then VGA then SVGA

CGI
COMMON GATEWAY INTERFACE
standard that defines how a WWW page can call special scripts stored on an internet server to carry out functions that enhance a Web page; for example, if a Web page provides a search function, the search function will be a special program that is called by the Web page using CGI commands
see also
PERL

channel
i) (in graphics) one layer of an image that can be worked on separately or which can be used to create special effects.
ii) (in MIDI music) a method of identifying each individual instrument in a MIDI orchestra: there are 16 channel numbers and an instrument can be assigned to each.

character
letter or number that is displayed or printed. The shape of each character is determined by the typeface and font that's used: each font includes 256 different characters normally with a to z and A to Z together with foreign characters, symbols and punctuation marks.

character generator
electronic chip that stores the patterns of pixels that form a character

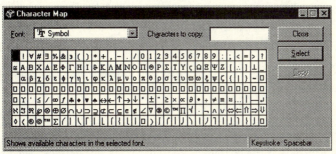

Character Map
utility that is provided with Windows to allow you access the full range of 256 characters that make up every font rather than the limited range that you can access from the keyboard. The extra characters include foreign characters and symbols.

character mode or text mode
operating mode of a computer or display screen that will only display pre-defined characters and will not allow graphic images to be displayed; Windows operates in a graphics mode, MS-DOS normally operates in a text mode

chassis
metal frame that is the basis for the computer system on your desk; the chassis normally has a number of devices attached to it including the motherboard, the power supply unit and the disk drives

chat

to send and receive messages, in real time, with other users on the internet; to chat to other users, you will need special software
see also
INTERNET RELAY CHAT

Cheapernet

slang term for Thin-wire Ethernet - because it is cheaper than Thick-Wire Ethernet.

checkbox

method of allowing a user to choose an option from a selection of possible options. The checkbox is a small box displayed; if you want to select the option, move the pointer onto the checkbox and click once, the box will now have a cross displayed inside it; if you don't want the option, click a second time and the box will be empty. The main feature of a checkbox is that you can choose several options at the same time. A radio buttons only allows you to choose one option at a time.
see also
RADIO BUTTON

checksum

number calculated from data that is used to make sure that the data is correct and valid; this is a simple process, for example if you are using a barcode scanner to read the barcode on the back of this book, the last digit is actually calculated from the other digits in the sequence and is used to make sure that the scanner reads the code correctly

child (window)

small window that's displayed inside a main window - often used to display options, for example if you want to change a font or check the spelling of a document then the options are all displayed in a child window.

chip

small electronic device that's at the heart of every computer and electronic gadget. A chip is a small thin piece of silicon crystal onto which is etched a tiny circuit with hundreds of thousands of components. These components will carry out simple mathematical operations such as adding and subtracting numbers (in a processor chip) or storing numbers (in a memory chip). If ever you open your PC (with the mains power unplugged, of course) you'll see a mass of small black boxes with tens of metal legs on each side: these are the chips.

circuit board

fibre glass sheet onto which electronic components are mounted and connected together to form a computer or other electronic device. If you open up your computer, you'll see one large cicuit board, normally at the bottom of the computer's box, called the motherboard

CISC

COMPLEX INSTRUCTION SET COMPUTER
design of a processor chip that contains a wide collection of instructions that makes it easier to program in assembly language, but its speed is generally slower than a

RISC processor that is designed to execute just a few instructions

Class 1, Class 2

standards that define how a to control a fax modem using software; the standard uses extensions to the Hayes AT command set used for data modems. Class 2 expects the modem to carry out more work in managing fax communications; Class 1 units can often be upgraded through software. Only modems advertised as "Class 2.0" follow the true Class 2 standard.

click

to press down once and release a key (on the keyboard) or one of the buttons on a mouse; normally used also to mean the action of moving the arrow pointer over an icon or menu or option and pressing once on a mouse button. Windows uses a click on the left-hand mouse button to select an icon and a click on the right-hand button to display a menu of options that apply to the icon (such as its name and properties). Wordprocessing applications often use different clicks to mean different things: move the pointer over a paragraph of text and click once with the left-hand button: the cursor is position where you clicked. Click twice and the word is highlighted, click three times and the paragraph is highlighted. If you want to open a document or icon (such as My Computer) or start an application then you need to double-click on the icon. A double-click is two rapid clicks on the left-hand mouse button; if nothing happens, try again making the clicks as short and fast as possible. One neat feature of Windows is click and drag (also called drag and drop). This lets you move an icon around the screen or move text in a word processor. First, move the pointer over the icon and press down on the left hand mouse button. Keep the button pressed down and move the mouse and you'll find the icon moves with you.

client

computer that is connected to a network or the internet, or a computer that is using the resources of another computer; if you are connected to the internet, your computer is the client and runs client software (such as a Web browser)

client-server

computing system consisting of networked 'clients' which request information and a central 'server' which stores data and manages shared information and resources. Client-server software, or architectures, are trying to reduce the amount of data traffic flowing over the wires between clients and server. It does this by processing data at the server as well as simply retrieving it. For example, a client PC with a simple front-end application asks the server to find all contacts in South London: the server searches through the database and returns the correct matches. The alternative is for the client to request the entire database to be sent which it then searches itself. The difference means that only the question and answer travels across the network rather than the entire database, which means that there is less traffic on the network

client-side

something that happens on the client's computer; for example, if you connect to the internet there are two ways of carrying out functions such as image maps and forms: either your computer stores the image and does the processing (called client-side) or the server computer does the work (called server-side); client-side is the usual method of implementing image maps

clip-art

library of pre-drawn images, drawings or photographs that you can use in your presentations, reports or desktop publishing documents. Normally, there are no copyright fees if you use the images for non-commercial use. You'll find that most presentation programs, such as Harvard Graphics or Lotus Freelance, come with hundreds of pre-drawn images, borders and icons in a clip-art library.

Clipboard
(in Windows) area of memory that is used for temporary storage of data; for example, if you select some text in a wordprocessor then cut it (using the Edit/Cut menu option), the text is actually temporarily stored in the Clipboard. If you choose the Edit/Paste menu option you can copy the text back from the Clipboard to the document. In Windows, the Clipboard can store any type of data: from text to sound, images, data and drawings. It is a very useful way of moving data from one program to another: for example, to copy your signature you've drawn in Paint to the bottom of a letter written in Microsoft Word, first choose Edit/Copy in Paint, switch to Word move to the bottom of the letter and choose Edit/Paste - your signature will appear. To see what is currently stored in the Clipboard, you can start a utility called Clipboard Viewer in the Accessories group in Windows. Almost all Windows applications use Ctrl-C to copy to the Clipboard, Ctrl-V to paste from the Clipboard and Ctrl-X to delete without copying.

clipping
to select an area of an image that's smaller than the original; if you are using the Paint program that's supplied with Windows you can use the area select tool to clip an image to keep the section of the image you want. The area select tool is the top right hand corner of the tools: select this and then move the cross-hair cursor to the top left hand corner of the area you want to click then, with the left-hand mouse button pressed down, drag the area you want to clip.

clock
i) tiny crystal in your computer that sends out a regular signal hundreds of thousands of times every second; it's used by all the electronic components to keep in time with each other so that data is not lost when it's transferred. The central processing unit normally carries out one instruction every clock pulse, so the faster the clock the more instructions it carries out. The speed of a processor (and so the clock) is measured in megahertz (MHz) which represent one million pulses every second: a processor that runs at 50mhz uses a clock that sends 50 million signals every second. ii) Windows 3.1 includes a utility called Clock that displays the current time in a window or as an icon: to start the utility, double-click on the Clock icon in the Accessories group. Windows 95 displays the time in the bottom right-hand corner of the screen. To see the date, move the pointer over the time and wait a couple of seconds: the data will pop up. To change how the time is displayed in Windows 95, move the pointer over the time display and click on the right-hand mouse button, this will display the clock setup screen.

clock doubler
special chip that works beside the central processing unit to double the number of clock pulses and so effectively double the speed of the central processor.

clock speed
frequency at which a clock runs in a computer or other electronic device. Clock speed of a processor is normally measured in millions of cycles per second (MHz).

close menu option
(normally under the File menu) menu option that will shut the document that's

currently open, but will not exit the application. If you have not saved the document, the application will warn you before it closes the document and give you the chance to save any changes.

cluster
smallest element that DOS (the operating system software that controls your PC) can read from or write to a disk.

CLUT
COLOUR LOOK-UP TABLE
table of numbers used in Windows and graphics programs to store the range of colours used in an image
see also
PALETTE

CMOS
COMPLEMENTARY METAL-OXIDE SEMICONDUCTOR
method of designing and manufacturing a range of electronic components; it produces components that are fast and consume little power, but are more expensive and cannot store as much information as other types of semiconductor

CMYK
CYAN MAGENTA YELLOW BLACK
method of describing any colour by the percentages of these four colours; normally used in high-end graphics and desktop publishing programs.

co-axial cable (coax)
special cable that is used to connect computers linked in a network. Co-axial cable looks like television aerial cable and is made from a central core of copper surrounded by plastic with a mesh of copper and a plastic outer covering.
compare with
TWISTED PAIR

codec
CODER-DECODER
electronic device that compresses video and sound signals before they are transmitted over a telephone modem connection or over the internet; the signals are decompressed at the receiving end. To achieve good-quality live video transmission over the internet, you need to use a high-speed codec that can compress the data and transmit it to the receiver

codepages
definition of the character that's produced by each key on the keyboard: the layout is different for different countries: the UK and the USA use the QWERTY standard (defined by the top line of characters on the keyboard), whilst France uses AZERTY and other countries incorporate accents and special characters. In order to use your computer when typing in a different language you need to change the keyboard layout and the font that's used for the characters - both are defined by the codepage. You can change the properties of the keyboard by opening the Keyboard icon in the Control Panel.

cold boot
to switch off a computer completely and then switch it back on again

compare with
WARM BOOT

collate

to print multiple copies of a document in correct order: if you want three copies of a document then, instead of the usual method of printing three copies of page one, three copies of page two and so on, the wordprocessing software is clever enough to print all the pages in order and repeat this three times.

collision

two signals that interfere with each other over a network, normally causing an error

colour

any colour displayed on a monitor is made up of three tiny dots behind the front of the glass screen. The colours from these three dots combine to create millions of different colours and shades that you can see. Although the monitor is capable of displaying millions of different colours, it's also dependent on the graphics adapter which has to control the electronics in the monitor.

colour bits

number of bits that define the colour displayed at each pixel location. One colour bit allows the pixel to display two colours, two colour bits can display four colours, eight colour bits can display 256 colours, 16 colour bits can display 65,000 different colours and 24 colour bits can display 16 million colours. Full colour or true-colour displays that can show photographic-quality images usually use 24 colour bits. There is a tradef off: the more colour bits you use for each pixel, the more memory this uses up. The number of colour bits that is used depends on the capabilities of the graphics adapter fitted in your computer; this has a limited amount of memory installed and can allocate this either to higher resolution display with more pixels or a display with more colours. A display with 24 colour bits will take three times as much memory as one with eight colour bits.

colour depth

number of different colours that can be displayed by any single pixel in a display - determined by the number of colour bits in each pixel.

colour palette

selection of colours that are currently being used in an image. Even though a pixel might have only eight colours bits, and so can display 256 different colours, you can choose these 256 colours from a range of millions of different colours: your choice of colours is the colour palette.

colour printer

device that can produce printed colour output on paper or film. The most common and cheapest colour printers are ink-jet printers. These use four coloured inks which are squirted in tiny dots onto the paper; by combining different coloured dots together, a wide range of different colours can be printed. Thermal-wax printers are the most accurate and the most expensive colour printers available. They use a tiny heating element to blend together four colour waxes that cool when they hit the surface of the paper.

COM

type of file that contains a program; COM program files are always less than 64Kb in size, wheras EXE program files can be almost any size. To view a list of program files that are stored on your hard disk, move to DOS (if you are in Windows, start an MS-DOS session) and enter 'DIR *.COM'; to run a COM program, enter the program name without the COM extension and press Return. For example, to run EDIT.COM type 'EDIT' and press Return

see also
EXE, PROGRAM

com

suffix on a domain name that means that the internet domain name is a company and (usually) based in the USA; for example, 'microsoft.com'; other common suffixes include 'co.uk' for UK-based companies, 'edu' for educational organisation and 'net' for ISPs

COM1

name used in PCs to represent the first serial port on the computer. If you plug an external modem into the first serial port, you are connecting it to COM1. There are normally two serial ports (COM1 and COM2) in a PC, although it can support four. Some PCs have a mouse plugged into the first serial port and the modem plugged into the second port. If you have connected a modem to a serial port on your PC you will need to configure your communications software so that it knows to which port your modem is connected by selecting the correct COM port.

command

instruction that tells the computer or a program to do something. For example, if you type in the command 'DIR' at the DOS prompt this tells the operating system of the computer to display a list of the files stored on the disk. The command to shut down the computer when using Windows 95 involves clicking on the Start button and selecting the Shutdown menu option

COMMAND.COM

program file that contains the command line interpreter for MS-DOS. Do not delete this program file if you see it on your hard disk or your computer will not respond to your commands .

see
COMMAND INTERPRETER

command interpreter

operating system software that runs on a computer and recognises commands entered by a user that control the actions of the computer. For example, in older computers the command interpreter was usually Microsoft's MS-DOS and translated typed commands into actions; in new computers the command interpreter is Windows 95 which translates mouse movements and menu selections into computer actions

command line

method of describing software that is controlled by typing in words. If you are used to Windows, where you point and click to make things happen, and think that this sounds strange remember DOS. DOS is command-line driven: to list the files that are stored, type in DIR, to change directory type in CD. To see what DOS looks like, double-click on the MS-DOS icon in the Accessories group of Windows 3.1 or select Start/Programs/MS-DOS Prompt from Windows 95.

command prompt

symbol that tells you that the software is ready to receive the next command. In

DOS, this is normally the 'C:>' symbol; to make this rather more friendly it's usual to include the path so that the command prompt might read 'C:\WINDOWS>' to indicate that you are looking at the C: drive and are in the \WINDOWS subdirectory. Since the command prompt is not very friendly and you have to remember dozens of special command words, it's hardly surprising that Windows was developed!

common gateway interface
see
CGI

communications software
software that allows you to connect to a remote computer using a modem to send and receive information. The software will dial the telephone number and displays information that's received as well as sending any text that you type in on your keyboard. Some on-line services, such as CompuServe and Microsoft Network, come with their own specially-written communications software that can only be used with this service. More complex communications software packages let you send and receive faxes and send and receive files.

comp
type of newsgroup that provides discussion about computers and computer programming
see also
ALT, BIZ, NEWSGROUPS

compact disc
see
CD

compatible
one version of hardware or software that will work with another type or version of hardware or software. For example, IBM designed the first PC but there are now hundreds of manufacturers that produce compatible computers that work in exactly the same way.

compiler
software used by programmers that converts a file of program instructions written in a programming langugage into a form that can be understood by the central processing unit. The final form is normally stored as an EXE or COM program file that contains machine code instructions to control the processor. If you want to create software you first write the program (either by typing in instructions or designing a flow-chart), this is passed to the compiler program that produces the finised application that you can then run.

compliant
device that conforms to a particular set of standards. For example, if you want to read PhotoCD compact discs in your computer you must be sure that the CD-ROM drive is PhotoCD or CD-ROM XA compliant.

composite monitor
colour monitor that receives the colour display signals from a graphics display adapter combined into one signal which must then be electronically separated inside

the monitor into the red, green and blue colour signals

compare with

RGB

compound document

one document that contains data that was created by other applications; for example, if you have a wordprocessor, you can insert images from a paint program or sound clips - the result is a compound document.

compression

to reduce the size of a file by encoding the data. For example, if the file contains five letter 'A's next to each other, which take up five bytes of space, the compression software could encode this to 5A which takes two byes of space. The compression software uses all sorts of encoding tricks to code the way data is stored to reduce the space it takes

see also

DATA COMPRESSION, PKZIP

CompuServe™

on-line service that provides hundreds of information sources that can be accessed by dialling in to the main computer with a modem. CompuServe is based in the USA and contains reference databases, such as stock exchange prices and weather maps, but it also has thousands of individual forums. The forums are each dedicated to a particular subject or product: for example, there is a Microsoft forum that covers each of its separate products (Word, Excel, Access). One of the great benefits of CompuServe over rival on-line services is that it has thousands of software and hardware companies that provide support for their products: if you're stuck with a problem, leave a message in the correct forum and someone will probably be able to solve it for you. Each CompuServe user is identified by a number or by a name, which can make it rather less friendly than other systems. For example, I am called 'Scollin' on one system, but '100373,675' on CompuServe; in

CompuServe software

order to be called 'Simon.Collin' on CompuServe I have to register my new name with CompuServe. You can use CompuServe to send electronic mail messages to any other CompuServe user, or to anyone who is connected to the internet. When you join CompuServe it sends you a special software package called CIM; this provides a simple way of accessing all the forums and reference databases on the system. CIM will dial the telephone number, send you user number and password and let you access forums and send mail. CompuServe charges in two ways: there's a small joining fee and then you are charged for the time you are connected to the service. In addition, some of the reference databases have an extra charge. Outside the USA you will normally also have to pay for the local telephone call

computer
electronic device that can carry out mathematical functions
see
PERSONAL COMPUTER

computer names
(in Windows 95) series of words that identify a computer on a network; each computer that is connected to a network is given an identifying name, if you are linked to an office network, you will see an icon on your Desktop called Network Neighborhood. Double-click on this and it will display a list of the other computers on the network, and their names.

CON
special name used in PCs to represent the console which is the monitor and keyboard; this name is rarely used

concurrent
two or more tasks running simultaneously on a computer; in practice this means that you can run more than one program at a time, for example to type a letter in a word processor and also checking the stock market figures from CompuServe and recalculate your company's profit margin in a spreadsheet. In an multiprocessor computer there are several processor chips, each of which can run one program. Most PCs use one single processor and achieve a similar result using Windows or OS/2 software: the operating system software switches very rapidly between each program. For example, if you are running the three programs mentioned earlier: Word, CompuServe and Excel, the software would divide the processor's time into tiny slices and give each a slice. This way, although the processor is servicing three programs, it's fast enough to look as if they are all running concurrently

condition
state of a particular electronic device or option; for example a check box condition can be either checked or blank. Also refers to the amount of electrical charge in a battery

CONFIG.SYS
One of two special text files that the user can create to configure the initial environment of the PC and load special device drivers. CONFIG.SYS is a file stored in the root directory of the disk used to start the PC (usually the hard disk if one is fitted or a floppy in drive A:). If this file is present, then the special commands stored in it are automatically executed when DOS starts up. The other startup file is AUTOEXEC.BAT which contains ordinary DOS commands and this is executed after CONFIG.SYS. If your PC is already set up, you probably already have an CONFIG.SYS file on your startup disk(s). You can check this with a

command such as DIR C:\ CONFIG.SYS. Use TYPE rather than DIR to show the commands that are stored in the file. You should be careful not to delete an existing CONFIG.SYS file or to make inappropriate changes to it as it may prevent software and add-ons from working properly. It is not necessary to have a CONFIG.SYS file. Without one, DOS will set itself up with basic defaults.

CONFIG.SYS is a plain text file that contains special configuration commands, with one per line. You can create or edit a CONFIG.SYS file using a text editor (such as Notepad or Edit).

The CONFIG.SYS file is often altered automatically if you install new programs onto your PC. It's used to load special device drivers and to setup any CD-ROM drives or networks or sound cards that are fitted to your computer. In addition, it is also used to setup and manage the memory in your PC - if you run the MEMMAKER utility, this will look in the CONFIG.SYS file and see if the memory is being efficiently used.

see also
AUTOEXEC.BAT

configuration

way in which a particular computer or software application has been set up and customised

configure

to set the function of software or hardware to your particular settings. You can configure Windows so that it displays a different colour background, or so that it uses a larger font that's easier to read. If you install a new software application there are two main steps: the first is the installation, which simply creates a new folder and copies the files onto your hard disk from the floppy disk or CD-ROM. Once the program is installed, you can configure it to work the way you want. For example, if you are adding Microsoft Word, you install it and then configure the way it looks and works. The Tools/Customize option lets you change the icons and menus that are displayed, whilst the Tools/Configure option lets you change the initial settings for the software. To change the way Windows looks, use the Control Panel. If you are using Windows 3.1x, open the Main group and double-click on the Control Panel icon; from Windows 95, select the Start button then the Settings option. Both display a set of icons that let you define the basic look and feel of Windows: from the speed and sensitivity of the mouse to the language used and the type of printer that's connected to your PC. For DOS users, the system is configured with commands stored in two files: AUTOEXEC.BAT and CONFIG.SYS.

console (CON)

keyboard and monitor in a computer system

consumables

extra materials that you need to buy to keep a printer or computer working properly; these could be a steady supply of blank floppy disks for the PC, and paper and ink or toner for the printer. These extras can easily cost as much as the basic equipment over the course of several years. When choosing a printer, look to see how much the consumables for this particular model will cost. If you are choosing a laser printer you will need to replace the toner cartridge (which contains dry, powdered ink) after a few thousand pages. After a couple of years of heavy use, you might also have to replace the drum (which is used to create the image). For an ink-jet printer it's cheaper, since you only need to buy new ink cartridges but these will only last a few hundred pages

contention

two electronic devices that are trying to send information over a network at the same time; one device has to stop to allow the other to transmit

context-sensitive help

type of help that displays information about the particular function that you are trying to use. For example, if you are using the search and replace function and press the F1 key (this is almost always the Help key), the software should display advice on using the search and replace function. If the software does not have context-sensitive help it would just display a general manual and you would then have to look for the section on search and replace.

control key (Ctrl)

key on the keyboard (in the bottom right and left corners of the main character pad) that is used for special functions. The control key is used with another key: press and hold down the control key and then press a second key and you will activate a special function. The keys and the functions all depend on the way the software was written: in many Windows-based applications there is a set of standard control key functions: Ctrl-S will save the current document, Ctrl-N will create a new document, Ctrl-P will print the document. You will often find that the control key is most useful in a wordprocessor when editing text: Ctrl-X will cut text which you can then paste back with Ctrl-V. In older wordprocessors, there was a standard developed by WordStar which used Ctrl-Y to delete a line, and Ctrl-T to move the cursor forward by one word. Don't try these with a Windows wordprocessor, because they use different functions! To move around any Windows application, Ctrl-right-arrow will move the cursor one word to the right, Ctrl-left-arrow will move it one word to the left; Ctrl-up-arrow will move the start of the paragraph, Ctrl-down-arrow will move to the end of the paragraph. Ctrl-Home will move to the start of the document and Ctrl-End to the end of the document.

compare with
ALT KEY

Control Panel

collection of icons that let you configure the basic functions of Windows and your PC. In Windows 3.1x, open the Main group and double-click on the Control Panel icon. In Windows 95, click on the Start/Settings button option. Within the Control Panel there are icons to define the fonts that are installed on your computer, the colour of the background to Windows, the type of printer that's installed, how a network works and a mass of other options.

controller

device that works as a middle-man, allowing a computer to use another device; for example, you need to fit a controller to support a CD-ROM drive

conventional memory

memory between zero and 640Kb. This area of memory is used to store programs when they are being run, together with device drivers and data. It's the main area of memory that is fitted in all PCs. However, because it's not really enough for the big software applications that are used today (such as Windows), most PCs are fitted with more memory - also called RAM. A standard PC would be fitted with 4Mb: the first 640Kb is still called the conventional memory, the next 384Kb is called upper memory and the remaining 3Mb is called extended memory. Luckily, you don't need to worry about how the memory is used: if you're using Windows 3.x there's a utility called MEMMAKER that will sort out your memory and make sure it's working at its best; for Windows 95 users, it's all done automatically.

cookie

tiny file that is stored on your computer when you connect to a remote internet site using a browser; the cookie is used by the remote site to store information about your options which can then be read when you next visit the site. This normally happens without the user being aware of it

cookie file

file that contains the cookie data supplied by the remote internet site; cookie files are normally stored in the same directory as your internet browser program

coprocessor

electronic device that works as a secondary processor to support the computer's main processor; a coprocessor normally carries out a range of more specialist instructions, such as mathematical functions or image operations
see also
NUMERIC COPROCESSOR

copy

to make a second, identical version of a file or section of text. If you copy a file, you make a second, identical file (use the COPY command). If you want to copy a section of text, highlight it then choose Edit/Copy, move to the place you want to add the copied text and choose Edit/Paste.

Courier

one of the fonts that's included with Windows and is also on almost every printer: it looks like a typewriter font and is a fixed width (also called monospace) font - each character is the same width, which makes it good for tables and charts.

CPU or processor
CENTRAL PROCESSING UNIT

electronic component that provides all the functions that control your computer and run software programs; a processor contains millions of tiny electronic components that have been designed to carry out basic arithmetic and control functions. A CPU can add or subtract two numbers, move numbers from one memory location to another or control an external device. It doesn't sound much, but it's enough to do everything that you see on your screen! Each of the actions of a CPU is controlled by an instruction - these are the machine code instructions that are used to create software programs. The specification of a CPU is defined in several ways: its speed (for example, 66MHz) roughly defines the number of instructions that it can process each second - 66 million in this case. The power of a CPU is also defined in its data handling capabilities: a 32-bit CPU can add, subtract or manipulate numbers that are 32-bits wide. A 16-bit processor can only handle 16-bit numbers, so would take twice as long to deal with a big number. Lastly, there are two main families of CPU. The Intel-developed range of CPUs is the 80386, 80486 and Pentium. These are used in PCs and are backwards compatible. Other manufacturers, such as AMD, are licensed to manufacture these CPUs and they work in exactly the same way. The second main family is the 68000 and PowerPC range from Motorola. These are used in Apple computers and are not directly compatible with the Intel range.
see also
COPROCESSOR

CPU clock

clock inside a processor device that generates a regular signal millions of times every second to control operations and data transfer within the processor

CPU clock speed

frequency of the CPU clock that controls the operations within the processor; the clock speed is normally measured in megahertz (MHz) - millions of signals per second. For example, current PCs have processor components that work at a clock speed of up to 200MHz

CR

CARRIAGE RETURN

code that (in a printer) moves the printhead to the left margin and (on a monitor) normally moves the cursor to the left margin and down one line. To enter a typed command you follow the command by pressing the carriage return key - also called the Enter key - which is on the right-hand side of the keyboard

compare with
LINE FEED

crash

event that occurs when a computer goes wrong and stops working. A crash can be caused by all sorts of problems with the software, but is normally because the computer has got itself into a terminal muddle or that the software you are using has still got bugs in it. When a PC crashes, the only way to get out of this is to switch off or reset (using the reset button or by pressing Ctrl-Alt-Del at the same time). Unfortunately, you will lose any new work you've keyed in since you last saved your work, so make sure that you save your work regularly.

crop

(in a paint or image editing program) to select and use a particular area of a picture. Paint programs all have a crop tool, which lets you stretch a border around the area you want to keep, you can then cut and paste this into a new picture. In some DTP software programs, you can adjust the size of a window that displays only a small part of an image - you don't change the original image.

crosshair

(in a drawing or paint program) shape of the cursor which looks like a cross. It's used when drawing lines or positioning an object.

CSLIP

version of the SLIP protocol that compresses data before it is transmitted, resulting in greater data transfer rate

see also
SLIP

Ctrl

see
CONTROL KEY

cursor

flashing shape on the screen that shows you where the next character you type in will appear. When entering text, the cursor is normally a flashing vertical bar.

see also
POINTER

cut and paste

to select a section of text or an image or other data, cut it from the original document (it is actually temporarily stored on the Clipboard) and then paste it at a new position or into a new document. To cut data, highlight the text or image and choose the Edit/Cut menu option. Move to the new position and choose the Edit/Paste menu option.

see also

CLIPBOARD

cybercafé

company that provides a shop with terminals connected to the internet as well as coffee and pastries; you can rent a terminal to try out the internet, and have a cup of coffee

cyberspace

world in which computers and people interact, normally via the internet; first coined by novelist William Gibson and now used to refer to the internet, its users and culture

Dd

DAC
DIGITAL TO ANALOG CONVERTOR
electronic device (that's normally part of a sound card) that converts numbers into sounds or other analog signals.
compare with
ADC

daemon
utility program that runs in the background and carries out a function; often used to organise files, search for information or download data

daisy-chain
to link several computers or other devices together in a daisy-chain fashion: the first is linked to the second, second to the third and so on. This is the system that's used in Ethernet networks and to link several disk drives to one computer - normally using a SCSI controller card.
see also
NETWORK, SCSI

DAT
DIGITAL AUDIO TAPE
small tape cassette that's used to record music or computer data onto tape in the form of digital numbers. If you use a DAT for music, it provides the same quality as a compact disc. DATs are most used to provide a backup of computer data since each tape can store over 1.3Gb of data.

data
collection of numbers, characters or symbols which are used by a computer. Once a computer has finished processing data, it presents this as information, which can be understood by a user.

data bus
collection of 32 tiny copper parallel tracks within a computer that carry the electrical signals that make up the individual bits of data from the CPU to the memory and any adapter cards.

data compression
techniques used to reduce the amount of data storage required to hold information; data compression is very important in modems, allowing more information to be transferred in a shorter period of time, and when storing data on a disk drive. Some methods of data compression analyse the data and look for repeating patterns in the data: for example, if the data is '1110011111' this could be reduced to three-ones,

two-zeros and five-ones (3, 2, 5) which might take less space
see also
JPEG, MNP, PKZIP, V42BIS

data encryption
techniques used to convert information into a form that cannot be read without the correct key; for example, if you want to send your credit card details to a shop on the internet, you should ensure that you encrypt the data so that only you and the shop can read the credit card details
see also
ENCRYPTION, PGP

data encryption standard (DES)
system of encrypting data developed by the US government and used in many security products and software

database
software that lets you enter information into one big, structured file so that it can then be searched. For example, a database could contain all your contact names and addresses or your customer details or your record collection. Each separate entry is called a record and each individual part of a record is called a field. For example, if you have a database of names and addresses, my details would be stored on one record, with my first name in one field and surname in another.
see also
RELATIONAL DATABASE

datagram
packet of data and a header that are sent over a network; the header specifies the destination of the data

date-time
current time and date stored on your computer; each PC has a tiny battery inside it that allows one area of memory to store the current time and date. If you need to change the time or date, use the Control Panel feature of Windows

daughterboard
type of expansion card that plugs into the main motherboard in the computer and adds extra functionality

daylight saving time
scheme that defines the changes in time over the course of a year; in the UK this means moving the clocks forward or backward by one hour each season. Windows 95 will automatically detect if the system time and date needs to be adjusted and warn you

DCE rates
number of bits of information that a modem can transmit per second over a telephone line (such as 14,400 bps); this is not the same as the DTE rate which measures how fast a modem can exchange data with another PC and takes into account data compression

DDE
DYNAMIC DATA EXCHANGE
(in Windows) system that allows two programs to exchange data. The two programs

must both be running and one asks the operating system (Windows) to create a link to the second program. Most major Windows applications support DDE; it's invisible to the user, but it does let you swap data between applications very easily - for example, you can use it within a wordprocessor to ask a spreadsheet to carry out a calculation.

see also
OLE

decay
shape of a sound signal as it fades away. The shape of the signal as it starts is called the attack, the main sound is called the sustain and then the decay is its shape as it fades. If you have a sound card and sound editing software, you can define the decay of a sound to create your own sounds.

decimal
number system used for base 10 with the numbers 0...9. This is the number system we use every day, but it's not used by computers - they have to convert all numbers into binary, base 2.

see also
BINARY

dedicated
computer or printer that is only used for one particular job. If you have a network, you might find that you do a lot of printing or need to store lots of files, in which case it would make sense to set aside one computer as a dedicated PC that looks after printing - it would not be used by any user, except for printing over a network. A dedicated terminal, for example, would be used to enter one type of data - maybe stock control or to type letters, it would not be used for anything else.

default
options that are used if no others are specified. For example, if you run a wordprocessor and start typing a letter, it will use the default font and typeface and the default paper size and margins. You can always change these default settings later.

deferred printing
delaying printing a document until a later time. This is particularly useful if you have a very long file to print - and you want to print it out overnight so that you do not hog the printer all day. To defer printing you will need a special utility or be connected to a network to set a new time for printing.

definition
ability of a display or printer to show fine detail.
see also
RESOLUTION, PIXEL

defragmentation
effect that is caused when a file is saved to disk, the operating system does not necessarily save it over a continous area of the disk. If the disk is full, it might have to split the file up and save it in several little chunks in different places. This doesn't matter to the software or to the user, but it does make it much slower to retrieve the file. If you think that your hard disk is slower than when you used it a few months ago, you could be right. The answer is to use a defragmentation utility that will reorganise your hard disk so that all the files are stored in continous areas

of disk and can speed up the performance of your computer. To do this, type DEFRAG at the DOS prompt

delete
to select text or other data and remove it from a file; to remove a file from your disk. If you delete a section of text, you can immediately undelete (using the Edit/Undelete) function. If you delete a file from your disk, you can sometimes undelete it depending on your PC's setup. If you are running Windows 95, there is a Recycle Bin that stores files that have deleted for a period of time - double click on the bin icon to see your file. In Windows 3.1x you can sometimes undelete a file by using the UNDELETE command from the DOS prompt.
see also
RECYLE BIN, UNDELETE

delimiter
special character or code that marks the end of a section of data, such as each field in a database record. The most common delimter in databases is the comma and Return code. Commas are used to mark the end of each field and the end of each record is marked with a Return character.

Delphi™
commercial online information provider that provides subscribers with access to its own databases and access to the internet

demo
trial version of a software application that shows you the main features, but has been crippled in some way - sometimes you cannot save the work, or it will only work for a few weeks.
see also
SHAREWARE

density
i) darkness of a printed image. If the ink or toner is running out in your printer, you will notice that the images it prints are not are dark as usual: areas of solid black are grey or streaked. You can sometimes adjust the density with a dial on the printer, otherwise you will need to replace the ink or toner cartridge.
ii) the amount of data that can be stored on a floppy disk; a single-density 3.5-inch disk can store 720Kb of data, a double-density disk can store 1.44Mb of data.

Desktop
(in Windows 95) refers to the icons and links that are viewed on the screen, when Windows starts up. The icons, status bar, Start button, Recycle Bin are all sitting on the Desktop. It's a rather odd concept, but probably easiest to imagine as if it were a real desk. On your desk you have folders, some open (the icons and windows), a waste-bin, and a small filing cabinet which is the MyComputer icon. The Desktop contains all these icons and objects, together with a background pattern and any windows or applications that might be open.

desktop background
pattern or image that is displayed by Windows as a backdrop (it's often called the wallpaper); your icons

Desktop of Windows 95

and program windows appear on top of the desktop background. To change the pattern or colour of your background or to display an image, open the Control Panel and select the Display which will let you change all the background options.

Desktop icons

icons that are displayed on the Desktop. There are two icons that are always on your Windows 95 Desktop - My Computer and Recycle Bin. If you are connected to a network, you might also see an Inbox icon which lets you send and receive mail messages. Any other icons are called shortcuts and provide a link to a program or to a document. You can create a shortcut to any file by highlighting the file (in Explorer) and clicking on the right-mouse button - you'll see a menu option that says 'create shortcut'. For example, if you create a shortcut to a document file called 'letter to boss', this will appear on your Desktop; if you double-click on this icon Windows will start your wordprocessor and automatically load the document.

desktop publishing (DTP)

design, layout and printing of documents, books and magazines using special desktop publishing software. DTP software allows you define the size and shape of a page, position blocks of text and pictures and manipulate the text to change its size, colour, typeface, leading and alignment.

Desktop taskbar

status bar that is normally displayed along the bottom of the screen in Windows 95. At the far left is a button marked Start, at the far right is a status display with the current time. If you click on the Start button, you'll see a list of the main activities: start a program, change the settings for your computer, get help or, lastly, shut down the PC in an orderly manner. If you have several windows or programs running, you'll see that each has an entry button on the desktop taskbar. If you want to switch to another window or program, just move to the taskbar and click on the button you want.The taskbar can be moved to the top or side of the screen: move the pointer over the taskbar (but not over a button) and click and drag the bar to a new position.

desktop video

combination of special software and extra hardware that allows a user to edit video on a PC. The hardware connects the PC to a video recorder or camera and captures the video frames; the software can then be used to cut individual frames, re-arrange the sequence of frames and add special effects or titles.

destination object

(in a drag and drop operation in Windows) when you drag and drop an icon in Windows, you drag it onto a destination object. For example, if you want to delete an icon, drag it onto the Recycle Bin icon - this is a type of destination object. If you want to start your wordprocessor program and automatically load an existing document, drag the document file onto the wordprocessor program icon - the program icon is another type of destination object.

device

electronic circuit that carries out some function; for example, a printer is a device, so is a serial port, so is a sound card.

device driver
see
DRIVER

dial

to use a computer to dial a telephone number, usually by using a modem (although a new telephony device can do the same). From your PC you can send instructions to your modem - which is connected via a serial port to the PC. The modem is plugged into a telephone socket and can be used to dial the access number of an on-line service or bulletin board (such as CompuServe), or can be used to take the grind out of dialling your friends and colleagues. To use your PC as a telephone book, you will need software that can instruct the modem to dial a number: In Windows you have a program called Cardfile that does the same job as a 'real' card index - the only difference is that it can automatically dial numbers via a modem; once the telephone is answered, pickup the telephone handset and carry on as normal.

dial-up connection

connection that uses a standard telephone line or ISDN link to connect your computer to an ISP or another computer; for example, if your main computer is at the office, but you decide to work from home, you can dial-up the office computer and access all the files stored on it or even log onto the office network and send messages - just as if you were there. To do this you need two modems, one on each PC, and the dial-up software that's supplied with Windows 95 (install the dial-up networking option of Windows to use this feature).

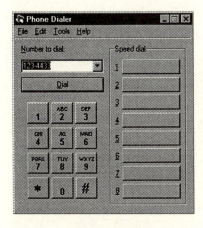

Dailer supplied with Microsoft Windows 95

Dialer (or Phone Dialer)

utility that's provided free with Windows 95 (it's stored in the Accessories folder) - to use it you need to have a modem connected to your PC. Dialer will dial telephone numbers for you, saving you the bother; when the person answers the phone, you pick up the handset and talk as normal

dialog

small window that is displayed in Windows in response to an action or to prompt the user for an answer; a dialog box is normally used to display a message (which could be a warning) from the program to the user. At the bottom of the dialog box are buttons: OK and Cancel are the two standard buttons, but there could be others depending on the message that's displayed. A simple dialog box might report back after a search and replace and just say 'replaced 23 items' with an OK button.

digital

refers to numbers and signals that represent a number rather than a continuously variable signal. For example, a gear box is a digital device since a car can be in first, second, third or reverse but not in 'first-and-a-half'. Compare this with analog, which refers to a signal whose value can vary continuously over time rather than taking a fixed values. For example, when someone speaks, the sound wave is an analog signal; it varies smoothly as the person speaks. PCs will only work with numbers so cannot directly deal with analog signals. To get around this, you need to fit an analog-to-digital convertors (A/D convertors). For example, a sound card contains an analog to digital converter to convert the sound signal from the microphone into numbers representing the volume. If a computer wants to create a sound, it must use a digital to analog convertor (D/A convertor) to change numbers into variations in volume.

see also
BINARY, DAC

digital monitor

monitor that can only show a fixed number of colours or shades of grey. The monitor accepts a digital signal from the computer and converts it internally into an analog signal. For example, early MDA, CGA and EGA monitors are digital monitors that can show just a few dozen colours.

compare with
ANALOG MONITOR

digital signal processing (DSP)

electronic device that carries out mathematical calculations on digital signals which have been converted from an original analog signal such as a voice, sound or video signal. These devices are normally used to create special effects in multimedia or sound cards or to enhance video or audio signals.

digital to analog convertor (DAC)

electronic device (normally part of a sound card) that converts numbers stored on a computer into sound

digital video interactive (DVI)

set of standards that define how video and sound are compressed and stored onto a disk and then de-compressed and displayed in real-time.

digitize

to convert an analog signal (such as speech, sound or light) into a numeric form which can be processed by a computer. For example, if you digitize speech you use an analog-to-digital converter to convert the sound into a series of numbers that can be stored on disk and then played back. If you digitize an image, you use a camera to convert the reflected light into an array of dots, each one a number that represents the brightness at that point.

DIMM

DUAL INLINE MEMORY MODULE
system of arranging RAM memory chips on two sides of a tiny expansion card that

can be inserted into a slot on the computer's motherboard to upgrade the main memory; DIMM cards are used to expand the memory in high-performance computers

see also
SIMM

DIP switch
DUAL INLINE PACKAGE SWITCH
small bank of switches that are used to configure a device

DIR
DOS command that displays a list of the files stored in the current directory.

direct cable connection
utility supplied with Windows 95 that allows you to link two computers together using a serial cable plugged into each serial port. The two computers can exchange files or share printers. The utility is particularly useful if you have a desktop PC and a laptop and you want to copy files from one to the other.

see also
BRIEFCASE

directory
method of organising files on a disk; a directory can contain files or other sub-directories. To imagine how a directory is related to a hard disk, think of the hard disk as a filing cabinet: each draw is a directory. If you open a directory, you'll see lots of folders (these are sub-directories). Look in a folder and you will see documents or files. In Windows 95, Microsoft changed the name for a directory to a folder

see also
FOLDER

directory synchronisation
way of ensuring that the files stored in similar directories on two computers contain the same, up-to-date information; normally used as a way of moving electronic mail from one server to another

disc
see
CD

discussion group
see
NEWSGROUP

disk
flat, circular piece of plastic that's coated with a substance that is capable of being magnetised and so store information. A hard disk consists of several rigid plastic discs arranged in parallel; a floppy disk has one thin, flexible plastic disc. The discs are spun by a motor at high speed and data is written to or read from the surface of the disc by a magnetic head (much like the one in your cassette recorder) that moves across the surface of the disc. Note, in computing you normally write 'disk' when referring to the storage device, or 'disc' when referring to a CD-ROM

see also
FLOPPY DISK, HARD DISK, REMOVABLE DISK

disk cache

high speed section of memory that is used to temporarily store frequently used data that has been read from the disk; the computer checks the cache to see if the data is there before it accesses the (much slower) disk and by using special controller software, this system can dramatically improve apparent disk performance

disk compression

method of increasing the apparent capacity of a disk to store data. The trick is carried out by a special piece of software that compresses the data as it is being saved to disk and then decompresses the data when it is read back

disk controller

electronic circuit that converts the requests for data issued by the computer into instructions that control the disk drive. In many PCs, the disk controller is built into the main circuit board of the computer (the motherboard) and will control the floppy disk and hard disk. If you want to add a CD-ROM drive, you will probably need to buy a special disk controller called a SCSI controller just for the CD-ROM drive.

disk crash

error that could corrupt the data stored on your hard disk; this type of error occurs rarely and is most likely to happen if you knock your computer sharply. During normal operation, the discs inside the hard disk drive are spun by a motor, an access head is used to read and write data onto the disc's surface actually has two tiny wings and 'flies' just above the surface of the disk. If you knock the PC, the magnetic head could wobble and touch the surface of the disc. If this happens, it will damage the surface of the disc and you could lose some data

disk drive

mechanical device that spins a floppy or hard disk and moves the access arm over the surface of the disk to read or write data

disk operating system (DOS)

software that controls the basic operations of the computer and the way in which data is stored on disk

see also
OPERATING SYSTEM

disk partition

see
PARTITION

disk tools

set of software programs that help you monitor the performance of your disk, maintain it and ensure that it's storing data efficiently and is in tip-top condition. If you look in the Accessories folder of Windows 95, you'll see the disk tools that are provided: disk defragmentor will gather up data that's spread all over the surface of your disk and store it neatly. Scandisk will look at every part of the disk and check it for faults and, if it finds any, will try and fix them. You should run both of these tools around once a month to prevent any problems.

see also
DEFRAGMENTATION

diskette
see
FLOPPY DISK

display
monitor that shows images or text

display adapter
device that controls what you see on a monitor. The display adapter takes instructions from the PC and converts these into electrical signals that define the colour, images and character shapes you see on your screen. If you have a graphics display adapter, such as an SVGA adapter, fitted in your PC then this will manage all the high-resolution graphics and colour and characters that you see on the monitor.

dissolve
special effect that is used in presentation graphics software or multimedia to fade out one image and the next fades in - it can also be used with sound segments in the same way.

distributed network
network in which each node can operate as a server storing files or working as a print server
see also
PEER-TO-PEER NETWORK

distributed processing
technique to enable processors or computers to share tasks amongst themselves most effectively. Each processor completes allocated sub-tasks independently and the results are then re-combined.

dither
i) to smooth out any jagged edges of a curve (for example, in a drawing or on a character) by placing shaded pixels between the pixels that make up the curve. Some graphics programs will do this automatically and some high-resolution laser printers will do this to improve the quality of the print.

ii) to create a new colour by displaying a pattern of coloured pixels that appears, to the eye, as a new colour: the eye blends the tiny pixels together and is fooled into thinking that this is a new colour. For example, a pattern of black and white pixels equally spaced would appear as grey; increase the number of black pixels and the grey darkens.

DLL
DYNAMIC LINK LIBRARY
file that contains part of a program stored on disk; the application loads the program code from the file when it needs it. This method ensures that program code is only loaded from disk when it is required. Large applications, such as a complex wordprocessor, might use several DLLs: one to carry out the spell-check, one to manage printing a letter and third for formatting the text. DLL files have a DLL three-letter extension and so are easy to spot using the Windows Explorer. Windows itself uses DLLs to carry out tasks that are only occassionally required - Windows stores its DLL files in the System sub-directory.

DMA

DIRECT MEMORY ACCESS

high-speed method of accessing the contents of memory chips in your computer; normally, if one device in your computer, such as a video card, wants to read information from the main memory it has to ask the central processor chip which then accesses the memory location and passes the information back to the video card. When using DMA, the video card temporarily takes over control of the computer from the central processor and directly retrieves the information from the memory. In the first case, the processor has to stop what it's doing and service the request from the video card. In the second case, the processor can carry out its calculations without interuption. To support DMA, you need a PC that's designed with a central bus (the electronic connections that link all the components together) that can support an intelligent video card - which in DMA talk is called a bus-master because it can directly control the memory and retrieve data over the bus.

DNS

see
DOMAIN NAME SYSTEM

domain

i) (in Windows) group of users, computers or servers on a network.
ii) (on the internet) name for a server or organisation on the internet

domain name system (DNS)

computer that stores the names and addresses of every other computer on the internet. This is used to lookup the correct destination address when you try and access a WWW page or send an electronic mail message. The DNS actually converts the name into a complex and unique pattern of numbers called the IP address which is then used to correctly locate the server within the internet

domain name

unique name that identifies the location of an internet server or computer on the internet. For example, pcp.co.uk is the domain name for the Peter Collin Publishing WWW server

DOS

DISK OPERATING SYSTEM

common operating system in use before Windows 95. DOS manages how files are stored on the disk; it keeps track of where the files are stored, how big they are and when they were created. It also provides time and date functions, together with the ability to start other software programs. DOS is controlled through a command-line interface, which means that you have to type in words to get it to do something. For example, if you want to see the files stored on a disk, type 'DIR' (short for directory). DOS is flexible and quick but is difficult for beginners to use because it's not in the least bit friendly. Microsoft Windows changed this by getting rid of the command-line interface and providing a graphical user interface in which you control actions by pointing and clicking with a mouse - there's no need to learn or type in command words.

see
COMMAND LINE, MS-DOS

DOS prompt

indicator that shows that DOS is ready to accept a command typed in at the keyboard; the prompt usually shows the disk drive letter and current directory, for

example 'C:\>'. You can change the prompt using the PROMPT command
see
COMMAND LINE, PROMPT

dot

full stop or (US) period, used to separate the parts of an internet domain name
(between the company name, type of site and country) and normally spoken when
reading an internet addresses; for example 'pcp.co.uk' is spoken as 'pcp dot co dot uk'

dot-matrix

type of printer that prints characters and numbers using a matrix of tiny dots of ink;
impact dot-matrix printers use tiny metal pins that press against an inked ribbon to
print the dots, while ink-jet printers fire tiny dots of ink onto the paper

dots per inch (dpi)

number of individual dots that a printer can print on an inch of paper. The greater
the number of dots, the smaller each must be and therefore the printer is capable of
producing sharper and clearer text and graphics. A laser printer can normally print
300 dots per inch both vertically and horizontally. Some bubble-jet printers can
manager 360 dots per inch horizontally, but only 200 vertically. High-resolution
laser printers use a variety of techniques to increase the apparent number of dots per
inch. For the best quality printed output, pick a laser printer with a resolution of 600
dots per inch. Some laser printers use tiny dots in between the main dots to smooth
edges and jagged curves, giving even crisper print-outs.

dot pitch

spacing between two adjacent pixels displayed on a monitor

double-click

to click twice in rapid succession on a mouse button. If you double-click on an
application icon, Windows will try and run the application. If you double-click on a
file, Windows will try and start the application that was used to create the file. A
double-click has to be done fast enough for Windows to realise what you are doing!
To practice, use the utilities that come with your mouse. As a tip, rest your hand on
the mouse with your finger resting gently on the left-hand button. Do two short
presses in quick succession. If you try and hold the mouse too tightly or press down
too far, you won't be able to double-click fast enough. If you move the pointer over
an icon and do a single click, the icon will be selected and you can change the icon's
name or properties. Lastly, a double-click normally only refers to the left-hand mouse
button, since the right-hand button is used to control the properties of an object.
see also
DRAG-AND-DROP

double-density disk

diskette that can store twice as much data as a single-density diskette

double-speed drive

refers to a CD-ROM drive that spins the disc at twice the speed of a normal drive.
The advantage of this is that the data can be read from the disc twice as fast (since
the disc is travelling past the read-head at twice the speed) and so you'll notice that
the response of multimedia titles is quicker and programs load faster. In fact,
double-speed CD-ROM drives are now the standard, for fast drives you need a
quad-speed or six-times speed drive!

DoubleSpace

software program that is part of MS-DOS 6 and is used to provide disk compression.

see
DISK COMPRESSION

down

computer that is not currently working, either because it is switched off or due to a fault

download

to copy a file from a remote computer onto your local computer; normally this means copying a file from a remote server over a modem link or internet connection or via a cable link from a laptop

compare with
UPLOAD

downsize

change in way a company uses computers so that tasks that were previously carried out by a mainframe or minicomputer are now carried out by cheaper networked PCs

downward compatibility

see
BACKWARDS COMPATIBLE

dpi

see
DOTS PER INCH

draft quality

printed output that is formatted and readable, but might not have all the illustrations in place or uses ragged typeface which are both faster to print

drag and drop

feature of Windows (and other graphical operating systems including Apple System 7, IBM OS/2 and Unix/X) in which you can move a highlighted icon or piece of text. For example, if you want to delete a file from the Windows 95 Desktop, you move the pointer to the file's icon, click once to highlight the icon and then press and hold down the left-hand mouse button. You have now 'picked up' the icon and can move it around the Desktop. With the mouse button still pressed down, move it to on top of the Recycle Bin icon - the Recycle Bin icon will change colour to indicate that it's recognised you want to use it. Now release the mouse button and you've deleted the file using drag and drop. In other applications, for example Word for Windows or other wordprocessors, you can highlight a section of text in a letter and then click and hold down the left-hand mouse button to move the section of text to another place in the document - or even to another document.

DRAM

DYNAMIC RANDOM ACCESS MEMORY

memory components that will retain information for as long as they have electrical power supplied; DRAM components form the main memory of almost all computers

compare with
STATIC RAM

drive

mechanical unit that holds a disk - which could be a floppy disk, CD-ROM or a hard disk - and responds to the instructions of a controller card. The drive will have a motor that spins the disk and an access head that can be positioned over the disk. The access head can, in the case of a floppy or hard disk, write or read data from the surface of the disk. In the case of a CD-ROM, the access head uses a tiny laser to read the holes etched in the surface of the disc.

drive array

multiple hard disk drives linked together with an intelligent controller that uses the drives to store multiple copies of the data on each drive for reliability or parts of each data on each drive for speed

see also
RAID

drive letters

Windows and DOS use a system of letters to identify the different drives that are fitted to the PC. A PC can have up to 26 drives fitted - one for each letter of the alphabet. Each drive is normally given a drive letter, for example the hard disk is normally drive 'C'. This is usually written as 'C:'. The standard configuration is: drive A: is a floppy disk drive, drive B: a second floppy disk drive, C: is the hard disk drive and D:is a CD-ROM drive. If you are connected to an office network, you might have other drive letters that actually map to a disk drive on someone else's PC. Lastly, if you have a very big hard disk drive, it might have been partitioned when you bought the PC. This means that the drive has been split up into manageable sections, called partitions. For example, if you have a hard disk drive with a 500Mb capacity, you might find it more useful to split it up into two sections each 250Mb in size. In this case, the first would be referred to as drive C: and the second as drive D:. If you added a CD-ROM drive to this PC, it would now be called drive E:.

driver

a special piece of software that sits between Windows and a peripheral and translates the instructions from Windows into a form that the periperhal can understand. In DOS, before Windows 95 arrived, all drivers were loaded when the PC was first switched on from within the CONFIG.SYS file. Now, a lot of drivers are built into Windows, although some will still have to be loaded from the CONFIG.SYS file - which is why your screen flashes between text and graphics mode when you first switch on your PC and it loads Windows 95.

see also
CONFIG.SYS

drop-down menu

a list of options that is displayed beneath a menu bar when you select a particular menu option. For example, if you select the File menu from any Windows application, a list of further options is displayed beneath the word 'File' - this is a drop-down menu.

DTE rates

a measure of how fast a modem can exchange data with another PC taking into account data compression and coding systems; the DTE rate is normally much higher than the DCE rate

DTP

DESKTOP PUBLISHING

using special software to layout text and images on screen, apply text formatting and special fonts before printing out the finished page on a high-resolution laser printer which could then be used as artwork for a commercial printer to print a book, brochure or newsletter

dual-scan display

colour LCD screen that updates the image on screen in two passes; dual-scan displays are cheaper than TFT displays, but are not as bright nor provide as crisp an image

see also
LCD, TFT DISPLAY

duplexing

technique to increase the fault tolerance of networks. In a duplexed disk system, there are two identical controllers and disk drives. Data is written to both via a separate controller. If one goes wrong, the second device is switched in under software control with no effect to the user. This is a more fault-tolerant system than disk mirroring.

DX

suffix after an Intel processor model number that signifies that the processor has a floating-point arithmetic unit, a 32-bit data path and a built-in cache; for example 80486DX has these features, the 80486SX does not

dynamic data exchange (DDE)

in Windows, a method for two programs to exchange data. The two programs must both be running and one asks the operating system (Windows) to create a link to the second program. Most major Windows applications support DDE; it's invisible to the user, but it does let you swap data between applications very easily - for example, you can use it within a wordprocessor to ask a spreadsheet to carry out a calculation.

see also
OLE, DLL

dynamic link library

see
DLL

dynamic RAM

see
DRAM

Ee

ECP
ENHANCED COMMUNICATION PORT

system developed by Microsoft to improve the performance and functionality of the parallel printer port; mainly used when connecting a laptop to a desktop computer via a parallel cable, or when linking your computer to a printer

edge
(in a signal) the fraction of a second when a signal changes from high to low or from low to high

edge connector
electrical connector along the edge of an expansion card; normally arranged as a row of thin metal strips leading to the edge of the card, an edge connector can be inserted into an expansion bus of a computer to allow electrical signals to be transferred to and from the expansion card

edge-triggered
(something) that is started by a change in a signal; for example, in your computer there are many devices that are activated by an edge-triggered interrupt - this means that they are activated by the change in an interrupt signal, either when it changes from high to low or from low to high

see also
INTERRUPT

EDO memory
EXTENDED DATA OUTPUT MEMORY

latest development in memory components that can provide better performance by temporarily storing the last piece of data that was saved to memory in a cache ready to be read back from memory; this means that the processor can read more data from the memory component within one clock cycle, so improves the amount of data that can be transferred

edu
suffix at the end of an internet domain name that indicates that the organisation is an educational institute rather than a commercial company

EEMS
ENHANCED EXTENDED MEMORY SPECIFICATION

improved version of the EMS specification that now forms part of EMS 4.0

see also
EMS

EEPROM
ELECTRICALLY ERASABLE PROGRAMMABLE READ-ONLY MEMORY

memory chip that can store data without requiring power (like a conventional ROM chip) but its contents can be erased by a special signal applied to one of its connections

see also
EPROM, RAM, ROM

EGA

an old popular standard for colour graphics that's now hardly ever used. It could display images at the highest resolution of 640x350 pixels and was superseded by VGA.

EIDE
EXTENDED INTEGRATED DRIVE ELECTRONICS

enhanced IDE specification that improves the performance and data transfer rates to and from a hard disk drive

see also
IDE

eight-bit systems
see also
THIRTY-TWO BIT

EISA
ELECTRONICS INDUSTRY STANDARDS ASSOCIATION

group of computer manufacturers that together defined an expansion bus for the PC. The expansion bus is called an EISA bus and is a rival to the MCA bus that was developed by IBM. Both types of bus allow expansion cards to take control of the computer and so improve the speed at which data is transferred between the expansion card and the computer. Most PCs have an ISA expansion bus which allows 16 bits of data to be transferred, the EISA and MCA buses allow 32-bits of data to be transferred. The advantage of EISA over MCA is that you can still use the older ISA expansion cards in an EISA slot, wheras an MCA expansion slot will only work with special MCA cards.

electronic mail

way of sending and receiving messages between users on a network. If you work in an office and all the PCs are linked together in a local area network, you could send messages to each user on the network. If you are connected to the internet, you can send messages to any other user who is also connected to the internet. In order to send a message, you'll need special software.

embedding

a feature of Windows that lets you drag a document, picture or sound into another document. For example, if you type a letter in WordPad and then want to add your signature, start the Paint program, draw your signature and drag it into the WordPad document. Embedding really means that you can include any compatible data object (such as the Paint file) in any other document.

EMS (expanded memory system)

system in a PC that defines the section of memory that lies above the 640Kb mark. Below the 640Kb mark the memory is called conventional memory and any program can use this. If you add more memory to your computer, you are actually adding expanded memory (since your PC will already have a basic 640Kb of memory fitted). If your PC has the usual 4Mb of memory fitted, the first 640Kb is conventional memory, the remainder is EMS. In order to make use of any EMS fitted, the software needs to be specially written - luckily, Windows can use EMS memory and so any Windows program can automatically use the extra memory.

emulate
to imitate something else. For example, a special piece of software running on an Apple Macintosh can emulate Microsoft Windows and allow you to run PC programs on a Mac.

enabled
function or menu item that is available to be used. If an option on a menu appears in grey text rather than black, this indicates that these are not enabled and that you cannot use the option. For example, if you are using a wordprocessor and have not selected an area of text, the copy and cut commands under the Edit menu are displayed in grey and cannot be used. If you now select an area of text, look at the Edit menu again and you'll see these options now appear in black and have been enabled.

end user
person that will use a program or product that a developer is creating.

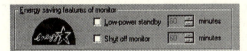

setting power conservation with an Energy Star-compliant monitor

Energy Star
standard and logo on a monitor, computer or other electrical device; the standard means that the product has been specially designed to save electricity: if it is switched on but has not been used for a while it will shut off some parts of the electrical circuits to save electricity. For example, many monitors will shut off power after five minutes of inactivity to save electricity

engine
part of a software package that carries out a particular function; for example, a search engine is the part of a multimedia title that lets a user search for text in a multimedia book

Enter key
key on a keyboard (on the right-hand side) that produces a carriage-return code when pressed by a user; the Enter key is used in a wordprocessing package to end a paragraph of text or enter a new line, it is used with an operating system (such as DOS) to execute a command
see also
CARRIAGE RETURN, COMMAND LINE

environment
electronic space in which you work when you use your computer. When you switch on your PC and it loads DOS or Windows, it creates an 'environment' for you to work in. The environment can be changed to suit your needs - by defining its

characteristics such as colour or wallpaper - and be setting up a printer, keyboard and fonts that you can use.

environment variable
special container within the computer's environment that holds information that a program can use. For example, if you are on a network there might be an environment variable set with your user name, another with the location of the program you are using. As a user you would not normally see or use these variables.

EPP
ENHANCED PARALLEL PORT
standard that defines the way data can be transferred at high speed through a parallel port connector (at the back of your computer); a standard parallel port sends data at around 150Kb per second, wheras an EPP port can transfer data at around 500Kb per second

EPROM
ERASABLE PROGRAMMABLE READ-ONLY MEMORY
memory component that can be programmed using a special electrical signal and it will retain this information even without electrical power; to erase the information, the component is normally placed under an unltraviolet light source
see also
FLASH ROM, ROM

EPS
ENCAPSULATED POSTSCRIPT
method of saving a formatted page or document to a file; the file contains PostScript page description commands. EPS is used as the filename extension for a file that contains PostScript commands - for example, 'PAGE1.EPS'.
see also
POSTSCRIPT

erase
i) tool in a graphics or paint program that sets an area of an image to the same colour as the background, effectively removing it - just like a pencil eraser.
ii) to permanently remove a stored file from disk.
see also
DELETE

error box or message
small window that pops up to tell you an error has occurred - for example, if you have tried to do something that the program does not understand, or if an error has occurred in the program.

error correction
technique used to correct any errors that have been introduced during transmission; high speed modems now have error correction systems built-in to ensure that the data received is correct
see
MNP, V42

errors
(in a program) problems caused by mistakes that have not been corrected by the software developer who created the program. In a commercial program that you buy

from a dealer there should be very few errors; if you do come across a strange error message, telephone the dealer and he can advise as to whether this is a bug or a mistake on your part. Bugs are the reason that software companies release patches (which fix a particular bug or error in a program - these are normally available free from the manufacturer.

see also
BUG, PATCH

Esc key

key on a PC keyboard, in the top left-hand corner, that is sometimes used to cancel an action. In Windows, pressing the Esc key is the same as selecting the Cancel button. If you press Alt-Esc within Windows you will cycle between any program windows that are currently running.

escape character

ASCII code number 27 that is used to send control data to some printers or programs

ESDI

ENHANCED SMALL DEVICE INTERFACE
standard specification that defines how a disk drive or tape drive is connected to a computer; this specification has been overtaken by the newer and faster SCSI-2 system

see also
SCSI

Ethernet

standard used for networking; Ethernet defines the type of cable, signal and language used if you connect several computers together. Normally refers to transmission of packets of data at 10 Mbits/second over co-axial cable with BNC connectors. It defines how the packets of data are formed, using IEEE standard 802.3; variations include the 10Base-T standard which uses twisted-pair cabling and various proprietary high-speed networks

see also
10BASE-T, CHEAPERNET, TOKEN RING

Eudora™

common commercial software program used to send, receive and manage electronic mail messages sent via the internet

even parity

way of transmitting data over a communications link that provides a very basic way of checking for transmission errors; the communications software counts how many '1's there are in each block of data it will transmit and sets an extra check bit to ensure that there is an even number of '1's in the data. If you are setting up your communications software to dial into a bulletin board system or online service, you will need to know whether the service requires even or odd parity. Most services expect you to use even parity - except CompuServe which often uses odd parity. Communications software packages like HyperTerminal in Windows 95 let you set the parity to either even or odd

event

action that occurs during the course of time; Windows works by responding to events. For example, if you click on the mouse button, this generates a button down event, then a button up event; if you press a key, it generates a key-press event, and so on. Windows waits for events and then responds to them - it won't do something until you tell it to do so. This type of program is called event-driven.

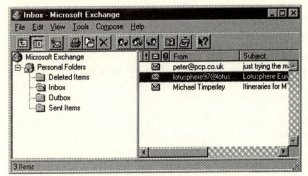

Microsoft Exchange

Exchange™
application supplied with Windows 95 that provides features that allow you to manage your communications including electronic mail and fax. Exchange can control a fax modem to send and receive fax messages; it can send and receive electronic mail messages with other PCs linked together in a network and it can send and receive messages to users linked to the internet via either CompuServe or a dial-up internet account. If you want to use Exchange to provide electronic mail for a small network then you can use the software supplied, however if you want to support several servers or postoffices you will need to upgrade to the commercial package, Exchange Server, that provides a wider range of features for larger networks and company sites

extended data output memory
see
EDO MEMORY

EXE file
three-letter filename extension that indicates that a file is a program and can be run. If you start a DOS window from Windows (or if you are already in DOS) type 'DIR' and you'll see the names of all the files stored in the current directory on your hard disk. To the right of the file name is the three letter filename extension that describes the type of file. DOC means document, WAV means Wave or sound file, EXE means executable - a program file that can be run. To run a file with an EXE extension, type in its name (you don't need to add the EXE suffix) and press return.

execute
to run a command or program on a computer

exit
to leave, quit or stop running a program on a computer. If you are using Windows, you can press the Alt key and F4 together to exit the program, or choose the File/Exit menu option

expanded memory
extra RAM memory fitted to your computer that is located at an address above

1Mb, but that uses special software to fool your computer into thinking that the memory is located below 1Mb and so can be used by any application. The special software that carries out the deception is called an expanded memory manager and needs to be loaded before you run any other applications. If you are using Windows it will work out for itself how it should best use the memory fitted to your PC

see also
EXTENDED MEMORY, MEMAKER

expansion bus
series of electical wires that carry the signals between the main processor chip in your PC and the other components, such as the video display card, the disk drive or serial port.

expansion card
set of electronic components fitted to a small piece of plastic that can expand the functionality of your PC. For example, if you want to connect your PC to a network, you will need to add the electronic components that control the way signals are sent over the network cable - this is done by buying a network expansion card. You can fit several expansion cards to a PC by plugging them into an empty expansion slot. To do this, you'll need to open up your PC: you can easily damage the sensitive electronic components, so follow the instructions in your computer's manual.

expansion slot
connector fitted to the motherboard that lets an expansion card connect to the expansion bus of a computer. The electrical signals from the expansion bus can be read by the expansion card.

expert system
program that lets a computer imitate an expert for a particular human activity. For example, some expert systems carry details of every type of medical symptom and link these to the cause. This means that if you, the patient, type in that you have a runny nose and a fever, the software will work out that this means you have a cold and not that you have sprained your back!

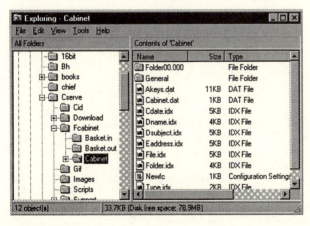

Microsoft Explorer

Explorer™
program supplied with Windows 95 that lets you manage all the files stored on a

disk. With Explorer you can copy files, move files from one folder to another, create new folders, and rename or delete files and folders. Explorer can also view folders on other PCs in a network. To start Explorer, click on the Start button, then choose Programs/Explorer. Windows 3.1x users have a similar utility called File Manager that's in the Accessories group.

export

to convert a file from its native format to another format so that it can be read by a different program. For example, if you have written a letter in Microsoft Word, and want to give it to a friend who uses Wordperfect for Windows, you need to export the Word document to a Wordperfect format file using the File/Save As option in Word.

extended character set

set of 128 special characters that includes accents, graphics, and symbols. Each font has a different set of extended characters; to see the range and to use a particular character in the set, start the Character Map utility that's provided with Windows. For the technically minded, the normal range of characters - A to Z, numbers and punctuation each has a code assigned called its ASCII number. For example, 'a' has an ASCII code of 97 in any font. The ASCII codes are only defined for the code numbers between 0 and 127. The characters represented by the ASCII codes between 128 and 255 are the special characters. If you want to enter any character into a document, in WordPad say, you can directly type in its ASCII code number rather than using the Character Map utility. For example, if you are writing a letter in French, you would need the é (e with an acute accent) character. This has an ASCII code of 233; to enter this, hold down the Alt key and enter 0233 on the numeric keypad, release the Alt key and the character will appear.

extended memory

section of main memory in your PC that lies above the 1Mb mark. The first 640Kb of memory is called conventional memory, the next 384Kb is called upper memory and any memory above 1Mb is called extended memory. The difference between extended memory and expanded memory is that any software program can use expanded memory, since it does not realise that it is using it (the memory manager fools the software), but software needs to be specially written to be able to use extended memory

see also
EXPANDED MEMORY, EMS

extension

(in a file stored on a disk) filename has the main name and a three letter code at the end that generally indicates the type or format of the file. For example, a filename in MS-DOS might be LETTER1 with the extension DOC; this is written with a full-stop separating the two parts of the name 'LETTER1.DOC'. The three-letter extension, DOC, indicates that the file is a document. Similarly, BMP means a bitmap graphic file, EXE means an executable program file and so on. In DOS and Windows 3.1x, the total length of the filename cannot exceed 11 characters, with a three letter extension this leaves just eight characters for the filename. In Windows 95 this has been changed and you can enter long file names.

external

something that is not fitted inside a computer's casing

Ff

facsimile
see
FAX

fan
electrical device that blows cool air onto a heat-sensitive device or that circulates cool air within a computer's case. If your computer is fitted with one of the newest processor chips, then you probably have two fans inside your computer's case: one glued on top of the processor chip itself to ensure that the processor remains cool and the other, larger, fan fitted to the back of the computer case to circulate cool air over the components inside the computer

FAQ
FREQUENTLY ASKED QUESTIONS
Web page or help file that contains common questions and their answers related to a particular subject

FAT
FILE ALLOCATION TABLE
data file that's stored on a disk and that contains the name, size, date and location of all the files that are stored on the disk. When you open a document in a wordprocessor, the wordprocessor asks DOS to open the file - it does this by looking through the file allocation table to find the position on the disk where the file is stored. The FAT is hidden, so you cannot see it, nor can you easily delete it - without it you cannot retrieve any of the information stored on your disk. Sometimes, the FAT can get corrupted - to remedy this problem run SCANDISK (a utility supplied by Microsoft with MS-DOS) or a commercial disk recovery program such as Norton Disk Doctor.

fax or facsimile functions
PCs can send and receive fax transmissions to and from any normal office fax machine. To send or receive a fax from your PC you will need a special modem that can handle fax data. If you want to send handwritten notes, you will also need a scanner - letters and graphics created on your PC can be sent directly via the fax modem. To control the modem, you will also need special fax software; Windows is supplied with several utilities that allow you to send and receive faxes (Windows 95 uses the Exchange program to receive faxes). If your computer receives a fax, it is stored as an image, which you can then view on screen or print out. If you want to send a fax, there are several ways of doing this: the easiest is to install the fax modem as a type of printer. If you want to fax a letter to someone, type the letter in your wordprocessor and select File/Print - you'll see your normal printer listed

together with the fax modem. Choose the fax modem and you'll be asked to type in the fax telephone number of the recipient.

fax group

method of defining the basic features of a fax machine or modem: groups 1 and 2 are old and rarely used now, group 3 is the most common standard used today, groups 3bis and 4 provide higher speed and better resolution of transmission

fax modem

modem that can be used to send and receive faxes to and from a standard fax machine as well as being used as a modem to connect to other computers

see also
MODEM

FDD

see
FLOPPY DISK DRIVE

field

(in a database) individual container that can hold a particular type of information. For example, if you have a contacts list of your customers, each entry is called a record and the various parts of each record are called fields - there would be a separate field for the name, address, telephone number and so on.

file

collection of information stored on a hard disk or floppy disk; the file has a name that identifies it and could be a letter, a spreadsheet or a program. To see the files that are stored on a disk, either type in the 'DIR' command at the DOS prompt or, if you are using Windows, start the Windows Explorer utility

see also
DIR, DOS, WINDOWS EXPLORER

file attributes

see
ATTRIBUTES

file format

way in which data is stored in a file. For example, every document created within Word for Windows is stored as a Word format file that includes special codes to tell Word how the margins are setup, the fonts that are used and if any images are included. Each type of program stores information in its own file format - this means that it's difficult to read a file that's been created by a different program to the one you are using. To get round this, you can either use the Import function of a program or use one of the standard file formats that let you exchange data between different programs.

file locking

method of preventing two users from trying to alter the contents of a file at the same time; the first user locks the file and can make any changes he wants, the second user must wait until the first user has finished using the file and has unlocked the file before he can make his changes. File locking is carried out automatically by any software program that runs on a network and is used by more than one person at a time

File Manager™

program supplied with Windows 3 that lets you manage all the files stored on a disk. With File Manager you can copy files, move files from one directory to another, create new directories, and rename or delete files. To start File Manager, open the Accessories group and double-click on the icon. Windows 95 users have a rather more sophisticated utility called Windows Explorer.

file properties

(in Windows 95) attributes that are assigned to a particular file, including its name, date that it was created, owner and so on which are all stored in the file's properties page. To view these properties, highlight the file with a single click from within Windows Explorer and click on the right-hand mouse button - now choose the Properties menu option to view the file's properties page

file server

see
SERVER

file sharing

feature that allows users on two or more computers connected via a network to access one file stored on a computer. If you want to share a file with other users on the network, you normally need to share the folder or directory in which the file is stored; if more than one user will share the file at the same time, you will need to set the file attributes so that the Share attribute is switched on

file transfer

to send a file from one computer to another, normally over a serial connection such as a modem link or cable between a desktop and laptop PC.

file transfer protocol

see
FTP

filename

unique name that identifies a file stored on disk. In DOS, a filename is made up of eight characters plus a three character filename extension that defines the type of file. For example, a letter might be called LETTER1.DOC. In Windows 95 you can enter long file names that are not limited to eight characters so the same file could be called 'Letter to Roger re proposal'. You can use most characters in a filename, except for a space. It's also possible to have two or more files with the same filename, but stored in different directories or folders on a disk.

filter

i) function in a database program that selects a group of records from the database according to a particular feature, for example, if you want to display all records where the country field is equal to France you would use the filter function (in Microsoft Access, select the Filter menu option). If you want to find a single record you would use the search function.

ii) feature of a program that lets you convert data from one format to another, for example, you can filter 1-2-3 spreadsheet files using the Import function of Microsoft Excel so that Excel can read the file correctly (in this context, filter is normally called Import).

Find

utility program supplied with Windows 95 that will search through any disk - on your PC or, if you are connected to a network, on any other PC - for a particular file, folder or computer; to use the Find function, select the Start/Find menu option

Find utility within Windows 95

finger

(on the internet) software program that will retrieve information about a user based on their electronic mail address; the program does this by asking DNS servers for more information about the location of the user
see also
DNS

firewall

security system fitted to a server connected to the internet; if you connect your main office server to the internet to provide a WWW server, or if you connect your WWW server computer to the office server without a firewall, then any user on the internet could gain access to your office server by getting around the very basic WWW security functions. To stop hackers gaining access to your internal office network via an internet connection, you should fit a firewall. The firewall could be sophisticated software that checks the address of each user that tries to access your server and blocks any unknown users, or could be a hardware device that prevents sensitive information travelling between the office server and the WWW server. If you are connecting your desktop computer to the internet using a modem, there is a very slight risk that someone could get into your computer whilst you are connected - but this does not warrant a firewall. If your office is permanently connected to the internet (for example, to provide electronic mail) then there is more of a risk and you should install a firewall system

flame

(on the internet) to send a rude or angry message to a user; normally in response to an offensive action, a controversial article, or a spammed article (an article that has been posted to multiple newsgroups)

flash ROM

electronic memory component that contains data that can normally only be read, but does allow new data to be stored in the memory using a special electrical signal; this type of memory component is now often used to store the BIOS or configuration information for a modem or other device. Normally, this configuration information is used to setup the modem each time it is switched on,

but if the manufacturer improves the features of the modem, the user can upgrade the functions of his modem by storing this new configuration data in the Flash ROM rather than replacing the chip or the entire modem
see also
ROM

flat screen
display monitor that has been manufactured with a flat, square-edged front to the monitor; older monitors often had a curved front to the display which meant that the image could appear distorted at the edges. To provide a flat screen, a monitor has to be manufactured using complex glass-blowing techniques and electronics within the monitor - which is why these monitors are often more expensive

flatbed scanner
scanner in which the original artwork to be scanned is placed face down on a sheet of glass; a lid is closed over this and the scan-head is moved (below the sheet of glass) across the artwork using accurate motors, converting the image into a graphics file that you can view on your computer. Flatbed scanners are more accurate than hand-held scanners and are normally more expensive.

floating point
system of writing a number using a decimal point; for example, '134' is an integer wheras '134.567' is a floating point number. These numbers are more difficult for a computer to manipulate so some computers can be fitted with a coprocessor chip that is dedicated to handling floating point numbers

floppy disk
convenient, portable storage device that stores information on a thin, flexible disk. The disk is coated with a magnetic material that's rather like an audio cassette tape. The information is stored on the disk as a series of magnetic signals using a disk drive. The flexible disk is protected from scratching within a rigid plastic case with a sliding window on one side to allow the disk drive access to the surface of the disk. There are two standard sizes of floppy disk - a larger 5.25-inch disk can store 1.2Mb of data and is now rarely used. The more robust and smaller 3.5-inch disk can store 1.44Mb of data and disk drives of this size are fitted to almost every new PC.

FM
FREQUENCY MODULATION

FM synthesizer
way of creating sounds by combining base signals of different frequencies; for example, sound cards using this technique create sounds of a piano, drum or guitar by combining different frequencies at different levels to recreate the complex sound of a musical instrument.
compare with
WAVETABLE

focus
i) to adjust a monitor so that the image that's displayed on the screen is sharp and clear.
ii) a particular window or field that is currently ready to accept a user's command - for example, if there are several check-boxes displayed in a window on screen, when you move to one of the check-boxes using the Tab key or mouse, this check-box is the focus and your actions control this particular box, not the others. In

Windows, the object that currently has the user's focus has a dotted line around it.

folder

container for mail messages in a user's mail front-end - rather like a directory under DOS

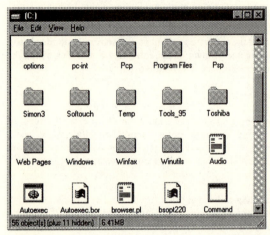

folders and file icons displayed in Windows 95

folder

i) (in Windows 95) name for a directory; a folder can contain files or other folders - just like a filing cabinet.

ii) (in an email application) container for mail messages that helps the user organise his messages; many email applications provide a feature called rules that allow the messages to be automatically placed in folders according to a set of user-defined rules. For example, if a message arrives regarding project X, a rule will automatically place this message in the folder for all messages to do with project X

see also
DIRECTORY, RULES

font

set of characters that are all in the same typeface. For example, labels in Windows are normally displayed in a font called Helvetica or Arial - the characters do not have serifs (the pointy bits on the edges of the letters). In Windows there are TrueType fonts that can be printed and displayed in almost any size, and printer fonts that can be printed in a range of pre-defined sizes.

see also
DOWNLOAD

Fonts Folder

(in Windows 95) location for all the fonts that are currently installed on your PC; to add a new font or to view the existing fonts, open the folder by clicking on Start/Settings/Fonts.

footer

information at the bottom of a page, typically the author's name, copyright, date or page number. Microsoft Word allows you to add footers to each page - select the

View/Footers menu option
compare with
HEADER

footprint
size of a computer's case on the desk

foreground colour
colour used to display text or information on top of any background image; for example, if you are creating a presentation, you might set the background image to a graduated blue with your company's logo in one corner. The text for each slide of the presentation is called the foreground text and would be displayed in a contrasting colour
see also
BACKGROUND

form
series of commands within HTML that allow a developer to ask a user to select choices or enter text; for example, if you want to allow a user to request a printed catalogue from your Web site, you would create a form with fields that allow the user to enter their address - together with a button to submit the form to the Web server for processing. In this case, the form processing would simply be to send the details by electronic mail to the network manager. Another example of a form is used by the search engines, such as Yahoo! and AltaVista; when you type in the words you want to search for, you are entering text in a form, which is sent to the search engine when you press the submit button
see also
CGI, HTML, PERL, APPENDIX

form feed
to advance the paper in a printer to the top of the next page or sheet; if you are using a laser or inkjet printer this has the effect of ejecting the current piece of paper

format
to arrange text and define margins, columns, include special fonts or embolden text in a wordprocessor or DTP program.

format a disk
to prepare a new disk so that files can be stored on it - you need to format any disk before you can use it: use the Format command from File Manager or Explorer.

forward
to send an email message that you have received on to another user

fps
FRAMES PER SECOND
number of individual frames of a video sequence that can be displayed each second to give the impression of movement. This number depends a lot on the power and speed of your PC. To give the impression of smooth, continuous (also called full-

motion) video your PC needs to display at least 25 separate frames each second. If the frames are small, there is not too much data to update; however, if the frame is large - for example, a large window display - then the PC has to update the hundreds of thousands of pixels that make up each image 25 times per second. To do this needs a fast graphics adapter or special video display hardware. If you want to experiment with video clips, start the Media Player tool and load any sample file that has an AVI extension.
see also
MPEG

fractal
complex geometric shape that repeats itself within itself and so always appears the same however much you magnify a part of the image. Fractals are used to compress images and to create interesting mathematical patterns.

fragmentation
problem that can occur when a file is stored on a disk: the operating system (DOS) normally tries to save it in one contiguous block. However, if your disk is very full, there might not be enough room to save the entire file in one block, so DOS splits the file up and stores the separate sections in any available gaps on the disk. This spread of bits of files over the disk is called fragmentation. It's not dangerous, but it will slow down your disk access time since the disk head has to move to several different parts of the disk to make up the entire file. There's a special program that's included with DOS and Windows 95 called DEFRAG that will go through the entire disk and sort it all out so that all the files are in complete blocks. You should try to run the DEFRAG program every month or so to keep your disk drive at peak performance.
see also
DEFRAG

frame
(in HTML Web pages) set of commands (developed by Netscape and now supported by most Web browsers) that allow the main window of a browser to be split into separate sections, each of which can be scrolled independently; most new or sophisticated Web pages use frames to present lots of information clearly
see also
HTML, APPENDIX

frame relay
communications protocol used to ensure that data is delivered correctly over a packet-switching system (such as X.25)

free WAIS
non-commercial version of the WAIS search index server
see
WAIS

front-end
part of a software program that a user sees and interacts with. The front-end has to be carefully designed to be clear, simple and straightforward to use.

ftp
FILE TRANSFER PROTOCOL
system used to transfer files between two computers linked via the internet or two

computers both running Unix linked via a network

see also

ARCHIE, BITFTP, TELNET

ftp mail

see

BITFTP

full duplex

two devices that can send and receive (talk and listen to) data at the same time; almost all modems allow full duplex data transmission over a telephone line, using different frequencies depending on whether the data is sent or received

full text search

to carry out a search for a word or item through the entire text of a database or multimedia application rather than limit the search to a particular section, chapter or field.

full-motion video

see

FPS

function key

one of several special keys running along the top of a PC's keyboard that have different uses according to different applications. For example, most applications use the F1 key to display help information and Alt-F4 to quit an application

Gg

gateway

(in electronic mail) software program or combination of server and software that links two different electronic mail systems together so that mail messages can be transferred from one system to another; for example, if you are using Lotus cc:Mail as the electronic mail product within your company, you would need to fit a gateway function to allow messages to be sent and received to users on the internet

gateway device

interconnection device that passes packets of data from one type of networking system, computer or application to another by converting the protocols and format of the packets used.

Gb

GIGABYTE

generic

something that is compatible with a whole family of hardware or software products from one manufacturer.

GHz

GIGAHERTZ
measure of frequency equal to one billion cycles per second

GIF file

GRAPHICS INTERFACE FORMAT
commonly-used format for storing images and bit-mapped colour graphics; originally developed for the CompuServe on-line system but now one of the most popular formats for images stored on the internet; most paint programs can read and write to the GIF file format. One extended version of the GIF file format, called animated GIF, allows several images to be stored in one file - these are then displayed in cycle and can be used to create simple animations (most animated or flashing buttons on the internet are created in this way)

gigabyte (Gb)

meaure of memory that is equal to 1024 megabytes of storage capacity; gigabyte is often wrongly used to mean 1000 megabytes

gigahertz (GHz)

measure of frequency equal to one billion cycles per second

glitch

minor error in receiving data accurately or a fault with a program

global
something which covers everything; for example, a global search and replace will replace all occurences of a word in an entire document.

Gopher
(on the internet) system that allows a user to find information and files stored on the internet using a series of commands; has been generally replaced by the search index programs that run under the WWW, such as InfoSeek
see also
ARCHIE, SEARCH INDEX, VERONICA, WAIS

graphical user interface (GUI)
interface between an operating system or a program and the user; this defines a way of representing files, functions and folders with little images (called icons). Windows is a GUI that makes it easier to operate a PC. Before Windows you had to type in commands at a command prompt to control the computer, with a GUI such as Windows you can use a mouse to point and click on an icon using the mouse rather than typing in the file name - which is far easier to learn and use. (GUI is pronnounced 'gooeey')

graphics
any form of pictures or lines that can be displayed on screen or printed out. Refers to shapes and patterns rather than to text characters

graphics accelerator
special card that fits inside your computer and uses a dedicated processer chip to speed up the action of drawing lines and images on the screen. In a normal PC, it's the main processor chip that has to carry out all the calculations to display a line on screen - at the same time as looking after the keyboard, mouse, disk drive and memory. By adding a graphics accelerator card you can speed up the reaction time of graphics software such as Windows, CAD or paint programs.

graphics adapter
electronic components on a circuit board that connected to the motherboard of your computer; these components are used to convert software instructions into electrical signals that control the text and images that are displayed on the monitor

graphics file
file stored on a disk that contains data that describes an image

greeked text
characters that are displayed as a dotted rather than individual characters; this is often used by DTP programs when displaying text in a very small type size. Greeked text is only meant to give an impression of the characters rather than a readable display

grid
matrix of evenly spaced horizontal and vertical lines that help you align and measure drawings. The grid lines are not printed but serve only as a guide in drawing or DTP applications.

grid snap
feature of drawing and DTP applications that will, when you are drawing a line or image, automatically limit the position of the cursor to a point on the grid, making it

easier to align drawings and lines on screen.

group

collection of files or icons within a separate window in the File Manager screen of Windows 3; not used in Windows 95

Group 3

see

FAX GROUP

GUI

see

GRAPHICAL USER INTERFACE

gutter

i) the blank space between two adjacent columns of text..

ii) the blank space or inner margin between two facing pages.

Hh

H
see
HEXADECIMAL

hacker
(originally) someone who was fascinated by computers and tried to program them as efficiently as possible or explore how they worked; now normally used to refer to someone who is trying to break into a secure computer system for criminal purposes - such as someone trying to discover a way into a bank's central computer.

halftone
way of representing tones in a printed image: a photograph is made up of continuous tones which a computer cannot represent, instead the photograph is converted into millions of groups of tiny dots - often too small for the eye to see - in which a group of small dots shows up as a light area and a group of large dots as a dark area. If you want to print any photograph, either on your laser printer or with a commercial printer, you will need to convert the photograph into a halftone image. If you are usng a scanner to read in the photograph to a graphics file on your computer, it will carry out this conversion automatically. In the case of a commercial printer, he will do the conversion for you before printing.

hand-held
device that is small enough to be held and used, such as a PDA
see also
PALM-TOP, PDA

hand-held scanner
small hand-held device, rather like a large mouse, that is used to scan small photographs and line drawings and convert these into graphic images that can be used on your computer. The scanner plugs into a special controller card in your PC and works using a row of light-sensitive cells along its bottom surface. When you move the scanner (by dragging it by hand) over an image, it reads the amount of light reflected from the image or photograph and converts this into a form which can be displayed on your computer
compare with
FLATBED SCANNER

handle
(in a graphics or DTP program) small square that's displayed on the edge of a frame or object or image; if you move the mouse pointer over the handle and click and drag with the mouse, you will resize or move the object.

handshaking

series of signals that are sent between two communication devices (such as two modems linked by telephone) to establish the way in which they should send and receive data.

hang

slang term that means your computer has stopped responding because of a temporary fault. Some programs, which are not tested thoroughly are liable to stop at unpredictable times and hang the computer. This means that you cannot do anything else except to switch off your PC and start again. Any data typed in since the last time you saved the document would be lost.

hard copy

printed document or copy of an image that's stored on computer.

hard disk (drive)

rigid magnetic disk that is able to store many times more data than a floppy disk and usually cannot be removed from the disk drive that's located inside your PC. In most PCs the hard disk drive is called drive C:, wheras the floppy disk drive is called drive A: or B:. A hard disk drive can normally store several hundred million bytes (or characters) of information, whereas a floppy disk can only store 1.44Mb

hardware

physical unit, hard disk, monitor or electronic circuit that is part of a computer system.
compare with
SOFTWARE

hardware compatibility

method of designing two different computers (or computers from different manufacturers) so that each can use the add-on hardware of the other without any changes. A prime example is the standard PC you are probably using - it is based on an original design by IBM and now all PCs are hardware compatible which means you can buy a network card or graphics adapter from any PC manufacturer and you can be reasonably sure that it will work correctly in your standard PC and that both the software and hardware will function correctly.
see also
BACKWARDS COMPATIBLE, EISA

hardware dependent

something that will only work on a particular type or configuration of hardware. For example, network software will only run and work properly if it can detect that a network adapter has been fitted into your PC.

Hayes AT command set

standard set of commands used to control a modem from a communications program; Hayes is a manufacturer of modems that allow you to send data over the telephone line to another computer; it standardised the software commands that allow a computer to control a modem and these commands (also known as the AT command set) means that any communications software can control just about any modem, as long as both are Hayes-compatible. For example, the command ATD123 means dial the number '123'

HDD
see
HARD DISK

head
special transducer that can read or write data from the surface of a magnetic disk. The head is just like the playback head in a cassette recorder and skims just above the surface of the disk as the disk spins using tiny wings that allow it to fly above the disk's surface

head crash
fault that occurs when the access head in a hard disk drive touches the surface of the spinning disk; a head crash is rare and generally caused by a sharp knock - such as dropping a computer - and will cause data to be lost from the hard disk

header
i) (in a document) text that appears at the very top of each page; for example, the header might contain the chapter name and the page number. Most wordprocessors and DTP applications let you define whether you want headers (in Word for Windows, look in the View menu under Header/Footer option). The line of text that runs along the bottom of each page is called the footer.

ii) part of a message that contains the recipient's address, sender's name and any delivery options

help
function in an application that displays explanatory text on screen to explain how to use the software or how to use a particular function. Context-sensitive help displays explanatory text about the particular control or command you are using rather than about the general program. Most software applications running under Windows on a PC link the help text to the F1 key.

help key
particular key on the keyboard that is linked to the help system of a software. Most Windows applications on a PC have standardised on the F1 key as the help key - press this key at any time and the software will display explanatory text that should help you understand the function or command you are puzzling over.

Hertz (Hz)
measure of the frequency of a signal in cycles per second

Hewlett Packard™
Hewlett Packard is a company that makes, amongst other things, a range of laser and ink-jet printers.

Hewlett Packard LaserJet™
brand name for a printer model produced by Hewlett Packard. The LaserJet has its own language called PCL that defined the way characters and graphics were printed on the page. This language has now become one of the two standards for sending data from a computer to a laser printer - the other language is called PostScript. Many laser printers are LaserJet compatible. This means that if you setup Windows so that it is configured to support an HP LaserJet printer, it will work with any LaserJet compatible printer.

hexadecimal (or hex or H)

hexadecimal is a way of representing numbers in base 16. Normally we use decimal numbers (base 10), but a computer uses binary numbers (base 2) which can be either a zero or a one. For convenience, computer programs and data are normally converted and displayed in base 16. Hex uses the letters A..F to represent the numbers 10-15 and if you ever see a number with an 'h' after it, such as 45h, this means that it's in base 16.

hidden files

your PC has a whole range of important and private files that you have probably never seen! If you list the files through Explorer or by using the DIR command at the DOS prompt, the operating system software will not show you the hidden files. These are files that have had a special flag set so that they are not displayed and cannot be easily deleted. If you really want to see all the files on your hard disk, use the ATTRIB command.

hierachical filing system

a way of storing files and folders within other folders on a disk. It makes it far easier to manage groups of files rather than storing all the files in one place - just like a filing cabinet which has different drawers, files and folders.

high density

floppy disks that can store either 1.2Mb for a 5.25-inch disk or 1.44Mb for a 3.5-inch disk; high density disks normally have an 'HD' symbol printed on one corner and have two sliding tabs on two corners. This differentiates them from double density disks that cannot store as much information

high memory area (HMA)

(small) area of memory in a PC that can be used by some programs. The HMA is 64Kb of extended memory that sits above the 1Mb limit and can only be accessed if you load a special HMA driver (which is done automatically for you when you install Windows 95). Note that HMA is not the same as high memory, which is a more general term that refers to a section of memory located between 640Kb and 1Mb marks

high resolution

screen or printer that can display fine images, normally refers to a display with a resolution of at least 640x480 or a printer that can print at a resolution of 300dpi
see also
DPI, RESOLUTION

highlight

to select a word or section of text in a document by moving the mouse pointer over the word and double-clicking on the mouse button. In Word for Windows, a double click will highlight the word you are over, a triple-click will highlight the line and a quadruple click will highlight the paragraph. You can tell that the text is highlighted because it normally appears in reverse (white text with a black background).

history

feature of some applications that keeps a log of the actions you have carried out or the places within a hypertext document that you have visited or the sites on the internet that you have explored. You can then return to any point you had previously visited by looking at the history list.

hit

i) action of accessing a Web page on your Web site.

ii) data that matches your search criteria

HMA

see
HIGH MEMORY AREA

Home key

key on a PC's keyboard (in the group above the four cursor control keys) that will move the cursor to the start of the current line. Some wordprocessing programs will move the cursor to the start of the document if you press the Home key twice.

home page

opening page of a Web site (normally stored in a file called index.html); if you enter a web site address into your Web browser, it will automatically open the home page. For example, if you enter 'www.microsoft.com' you will actually see the home page of this site that is stored in a file called index.html.

hop

path taken by a packet of data as it moves from one server or router to another; when you send information over the internet (or a wide area network) your data will probably have to travel via several servers to reach its destination

horizontal scroll bar

bar displayed along the bottom of a window that indicates that there is more information than can be displayed in the window. You can move horizontally to display the rest of the information by clicking on the arrow buttons at each end of the scroll bar.

host

computer that stores the Web site you want to access; the host will have its own IP address and a domain name

host adapter

device that is used to control SCSI devices; for example, if you want to add a CD-ROM drive to your computeryou will also need to install a special controller card (that is called the host adapter)

host name

name given to a web site on the internet; for example, www.pcp.co.uk is the host name for the Peter Collin Publishing web site. When you type in this host name, also called the site address, the text is converted by a DNS server to a complex address that uniquely identifies the site

see also
DNS

hot key

way of selecting a menu option or command by pressing two or more keys at the same time. For example, instead of selecting the File/Save menu option, most Windows programs use a hot key shortcut of Alt-S (the Alt key and the S key pressed at the same time) to do the same thing. Another useful hot key shortcut is Alt-F4 which will quit any Windows program.

hotspot

(in a multimedia title) area of an image that does something if you move the mouse pointer onto the area and click on the mouse button. Normally, you can tell that there is a hotspot in an image because the mouse pointer changes shape from an arrow to a hand. For example, if the multimedia title displayed a picture of a guitar, there could be a hotspot over each string which would play the sound of the string being plucked when you clicked on the hotspot.

HP

see
HEWLETT PACKARD

HP-PCL

series of commands (developed by Hewlett Packard) that allows any application to control any of the HP range of printers. This set of commands, or language, is built into all the LaserJet and DeskJet printers. If you buy a printer that is LaserJet-compatible and your software does not directly support this particular printer, set the software to HP LaserJet mode

HTML

HYPERTEXT MARKUP LANGUAGE
series of special codes that define the typeface and style that should be used when displaying the text and also allow hypertext links to other parts of the document or to other documents. HTML is normally used to create documents for the World Wide Web - the graphical part of the internet. A document coded in HTML can be displayed on any viewer software that understands HTML - such as a WWW browser. Note, for a full list of all the HTML tags, see the Appendix.
see also
BROWSER, INDEX PAGE, HYPERTEXT, WWW

HTTP

HYPERTEXT TRANSFER PROTOCOL
commands used by a browser to ask an internet Web server for information about a Web page; when you enter a site name into your browser (for example, www.pcp.co.uk) the browser then has a conversation with the remote Web server and asks it to send the file that contains the home page; this conversation is carried out using HTTP commands and the remote server that is being asked questions by your browser is called an HTTP server

HTTPD

HYPERTEXT TRANSFER PROTOCOL DAEMON
Web server that carries out the functions required to process forms, image maps, authentication and searching

hub

device that connects together several terminals or computers to form an electrical network allowing data to transfer between each device; for example, if you want to connect ten computers together in your office, you would probably use 10BaseT cable to link each computer to a small box called the hub. The hub creates an electrical connection between each computer

HyperTerminal

(in Windows 95) communications program that is included with Windows 95 and allows you call a remote computer via a modem and transfer files. It's not meant to be used to access the internet, it's more useful when used to access bulletin boards or other on-line services.

hyperlink

word or image or button in a Web page or multimedia title that moves the user to another page when clicked

hypertext

i) (internet) a way of linking one word or image to another page; when the user selects the word or image, he jumps directly to the new page. This is the basis of navigating around the WWW - if you click on an underlined word in a Web page, it will link you to another section of the page or to another page.

ii) (multimedia) a way of organising information in a multimedia title: certain words in the text include a link to another part of the book or to another document. When the user clicks on the word, he is moved to another part of the document or book.

hypertext markup language

see
HTML

hyphenation and justification

feature of most wordprocessing and DTP programs that will align a line of text so that both ends are level with the left and right margins. It will either split a long word over two lines (hyphenation) or will add tiny spaces between words to pad a line to fit.

hypertext transfer protocol

see
HTTP

hypertext transfer protocol daemon

see
HTTPD

Hz

see
HERTZ

Ii

I-beam cursor
(in Windows) flashing cursor shaped like a capital letter 'I' and used to indicate that you are can edit text on screen. For example, if you use a Windows wordprocessor, the mouse pointer turns into an I-beam cursor when you move it over the main page and returns to an arrow shape when you move it over the menu bar or other controls.

IBM
currently, the biggest computer company in the world, IBM developed the first PC based on an Intel processor and now sells a range of desktop and laptop computers as well as its traditional large mainframe computers.

IC
see
INTEGRATED CIRCUIT

icon
(in a GUI, such as Windows) small graphic symbol or picture that's displayed on screen and used to identify a command or file. For example, many wordprocessors use an icon of a magnifying glass on a button to indicate that this button will start a search function. Within Windows, each application you install has its own program icon and its data files often use the same icon - for example, the Microsoft Excel program has a large X as its icon that is displayed in Explorer or FileManager.

IDE
INTEGRATED DRIVE ELECTRONICS
standard that defines the way in which a hard disk and its controller connect together and operate. Most home PCs are fitted with an IDE controller and IDE-compatible hard disk drive within the casing. This is not normally important until you want to expand your hard disk capacity or add another disk drive. PCs used as network servers or those used for power tasks, such as CAD, often use the rival SCSI standard that is more powerful than the IDE standard. The two, naturally, are not compatible.

IE
see
INTERNET EXPLORER

IIS
INTERNET INFORMATION SERVER™
internet Web server software developed by Microsoft

image editor
software that lets you edit, change or paint new parts of an image. For example, professional designers might use an image editor to remove any blemishes from a photograph that has been scanned in. Windows has its own basic image editor (that is also a paint program), called Paint - it's stored in the Accessories folder.

import
(in an application) function that allows you to use a data file produced by another program and stored in another format in your application. For example, if you use Microsoft Word and want to read a document written with WordPerfect, you will need to choose the import menu option in Word and tell Word that it should convert the WordPerfect codes to native Word codes and formats. The opposite is export.

InBox
(in Windows 95) feature of the Windows messaging system (Exchange) that can gather together all your electronic messages including mail sent over the network, fax messages and mail sent over the internet. All these messages are stored in your personal InBox. Once you have installed Exchange you'll see a new icon on your Desktop called InBox; double-click on InBox to send messages or to read new messages.

index
list of subjects with related Web sites

index.html
filename that is normally used to store the home page on any Web site on the internet
see
HOMEPAGE

industry standard architecture
see
ISA

infra-red link
system that allows two computers or a computer and a printer to exchange information using an infra-red light beam to carry the data. Many new laptop computers now have an infra-red connector that allows you to exchange information with a desktop or printer without having to use cables

initialization string
series of AT commands sent to a modem to configure it before it is used

ink
(in a paint or design program) colour that will be used when drawing; most paint programs display two colours on screen - one is the ink, the other is the paper: the ink is the colour when drawing and the paper is the colour used when erasing a part of a drawing. You can normally change the ink to any other colour in the palette.

ink-jet printer
light, quiet and relatively cheap printer that produces printed output by sending a stream of tiny drops of electrically charged ink to the surface of the the the paper. The movement of the drops of ink is controlled by an electrical field to define the shape of each character, drop by drop. There are few moving parts (hence it's very quiet)

but the quality, although better than a dot-matrix printer, is not as good nor as fast as a laser printer.

inline plug-in
see
PLUG-IN

input
to transfer information into a computer; for example, if you type text on your keyboard you are actually inputting data into the computer. Another example is to use a scanner or to use a mouse to draw on screen - both are examples of computer input.

Ins key
key on a PC's keyboard that switches the typing mode between insert and overwrite. If you are in overwrite mode, any existing characters will be overwritten with the new text you type in. If you are in insert mode any existing characters are moved along automatically to make space for the new characters. Most wordprocessors tell you which mode you are in by displaying 'OVR' for overwrite and 'INS' for insert in the status bar at the bottom of the screen.

install
process of copying and setting up an application program onto your hard disk. The steps normally include copying the files from the floppy disks or CD-ROM (on which the application is sold) onto your hard disk, then configuring the options for your requirements.

integer
mathematical term used to describe a whole number, such as 12, 135 or 987. An integer cannot have fractions or decimal points. You might come across integers in DTP programs or CAD software.

integral
feature or hardware device that is already built into the program or computer. For example, most computers are fitted with a floppy disk and internal hard disk drive as standard. Both these are integral to the computer system. In the case of a software feature, an example would be the Exchange utility within Windows - this provides messaging as an integral part of Windows 95.

integrated circuit (IC)
tiny electronic device consisting of a small piece of a crystal of a semiconductor onto which are etched a number of microscopic electronic components. Together, these electronic components form a circuit which carries out a function. For example, the central processor of a computer is a very complex integrated circuit that can perform mathematical operations on numbers.

integrated drive electronics
see
IDE

integrated services digital network
see
ISDN

Intel

company that manufactures integrated circuit components and was the first
company to develop a commercially available microprocessor (the 4004); Intel also
develops the range of 80x86 processors and the Pentium processor that are used in
many PCs.

intelligent

software program that can respond to situations in a similar (although limited) way
to that of a human. For example, some doctors now use computers that ask the
patient simple questions and can deduce the possible ailment and treatment - this is
a basic form of intelligence.

interactive

multimedia title that allows the user to control the progress through the book.
Instead of the software showing page one, then two, three and so on, the user can
move around and click on hypertext links and hotspots that move him around the
book in a random order

interface

see
GUI

interlace

method of building up an image on a display using two passes over the entire screen
- each pass displays alternate lines. Although this system requires two passes, each
only displays half the information in a shorter time than one complete pass, so
reducing the appearance of flicker.

interleave

method of storing data on alternate tracks on a hard disk drive to slow down data
transfer rates to match a slower processor. Many hard disks store information in
non-consecutive sectors on the disk; for example a file might be stored in sectors
100, 102, 104 and 106. Hard disks are configured with an interleave to slow down
their performance and allow a slower computer to keep up with the amount of data
that is being transferred. The number of sectors skipped is called the interleave
factor; for example, a disk drive saving a file to sectors 4, 6, 8, 10 has an interleave
factor of two. Fast computers run the hard disk with no interleave factor, since they
can cope with the fast flow of data to and from the hard disk.

internal

(something) inside the computer or inside the computer's case
compare with
EXTERNAL

international standards organisation

see
ISO

internet

international network that links together thousands of computers using telephone
and cable links; these computers are called the servers and are rather like a local
telephone exchange - individual users can then use a modem to connect to the
server computer from their home and so have access to the entire world network. A
user can send electronic mail over the internet and transfer files and text from one

computer in London to another in New York - all for the price of a local phone call to your nearest server. The World Wide Web is an enhancement to the internet and provides a graphical front-end to the different databases and servers that are available. In order to connect to the internet, you'll need a modem and an account with a server - normally called an internet service provider (ISP) or point-of-presence provider - together with some special software. You'll be given a unique ID name that will (like your telephone number) identify you to any other user in the world together with an access telephone number that allows your modem to connect to their server. No one person or company controls the internet.

see also
DIALUP, DNS, ISP, WWW

internet Explorer™ (IE)

Web browser developed by Microsoft, currently available free, that allows a user to view Web pages; it supports many features including ActiveX applets. To download a copy, visit the Microsoft WWW site: http://www.microsoft.com.

compare with
NETSCAPE

internet Information Server™ (IIS)

internet Web server software developed by Microsoft

internet relay chat

see
IRC

internet service provider

see
ISP

InterNIC

organisation that manages the way domain names are assigned to companies

interrupt

electronic signal that diverts the central processor in your computer from one task to another. For example, if the processor is looking after the printer and you move your mouse, this will generate an interrupt signal that tells the processor to look after the mouse actions.

interrupt request

see
IRQ

intranet

private network of computers within a company that provide similar functions to the internet - such as electronic mail, newsgroups and the WWW, but do not have the associated security risks of making the information public or linking the company to a public network

invalid

input to a program that is not appropriate. For example, if you are prompted to enter the date and you enter a name by mistake, this invalid response will be rejected.

IP

unique number that defines a computer that is connected to the internet. Each time you connect to the internet you use an IP number that identifies you; the IP number is a 32-bit number normally written separated by full stops, such as: 132.167.9.223
see also
DNS, TCP/IP

IRC

INTERNET RELAY CHAT
system that allows many users to participate in a chat session in which each user can send messages and sees the text of any other user

IRQ

INTERRUPT REQUEST
signal from a device to the central processor that asks the processor to stop what it is doing and look after the needs of the signalling device

ISA

INDUSTRY STANDARD ARCHITECTURE
standard method of designing the expansion bus within a computer that allows any compatible expansion card to work in any PC that has an ISA bus. The ISA bus was the only bus design used in almost all PC-compatible computers and is sometimes called an AT bus and transfers data 16 bits at a time, which slows down newer faster processors that work with 32 bits of data. Because of this, this bus has been superseded by bus designs that provide faster data transfer
see also
EISA, LOCAL BUS, PCI, MCA

ISDN

INTEGRATED SERVICES DIGITAL NETWORK
system that allows data and voice signals to be transmitted over a digital telephone line using an ISDN adapter. ISDN normally transmits data at 64Kbps - much faster than a normal modem - and makes a call and connects very quickly: you can dial and connect within a tenth of second using ISDN, wheras it could take over a minute using a traditional analog telephone line. An ISDN connection works in a similar way to a normal telephone call: you dial the ISDN telephone number and connect, this is different from a leased line that provides a permanent digital link between two points
see also
LEASED LINE

ISO OSI reference model

INTERNATIONAL STANDARDS ORGANISATION OPEN STANDARDS INTERCONNECT
official definition of the way a network is organised; the definition describes seven layers of network function from the lowest layer (physical), which deals with physical connections such as the wires, connectors and electrical signals; to the highest layer (application), which provides the user interface to the lower levels. OSI offers guidelines for developers enabling them to design networks and related products which can talk, regardless of their make and use.

ISP

INTERNET SERVICE PROVIDER
company that provides one of the permanent links that make up the internet and

sells connections to private users and companies to allow them to access the internet. If you want to access the internet you will (in most cases) have to have an account with an ISP. The ISP normally has very fast fixed links to other ISPs on the internet and provides telephone access numbers for users to dial in with a modem or ISDN adapter. When you subscribe to an ISP you will be assigned a user name which will be your electronic mail address; for example, if you have an account with the XYZ ISP company, you might have a mail address of 'simon.collin@xyz.co.uk'. The ISP will also provide a list of telephone access numbers (called POPs - points of presence) that are used to dial into the ISP's computer using your modem. In order to connect to the internet, you will need a dialer utility that dials the telephone access number, a TCP/IP protocol stack (often called a socket driver) and a Web browser or electronic mail program.

Jj

jack

connector plug that has one central pin; usually used to connect audio equipment - for example, a microphone or speakers are connected to a sound card using a jack plug

jaggies

slang term for the jagged edges that you'll see along the sides of curves, graphics or round characters. Jaggies occur because the printer can only print individual dots rather than smooth lines.

Java™

programming language and program definition developed by Sun Microsystems used to create small applications designed to enhance the functionality of a Web page; for example, if you want to add multimedia effects to your Web page, you cannot carry out these functions with standard HTML commands, so you could write a small Java program, called an applet, that is automatically downloaded by the user's browser and run on the user's computer. In order to run a Java applet, the user needs a Web browser that supports Java, such as Microsoft IE 3 or Netscape Navigator. A Java applet is a self-contained program file that is downloaded separately from the Web page and run on the user's computer; a JavaScript program is a series of commands included within a Web page HTML file and executed by the Web browser.

see also
ACTIVEX APPLET, VBSCRIPT

JavaScript™

set of programming commands that can be included within a normal Web page (that is written using HTML commands); the JavaScript commands carry out a function to enhance the Web page - such as providing the time of day, animation or form processing. A Java applet is a self-contained program file that is downloaded separately from the Web page and run on the user's computer; a JavaScript program is a series of commands included within a Web page HTML file and executed by the Web browser. To write JavaScript you need to learn the script commands and then use an editor to add them to your Web page file; to create a Java application you need a program compiler and programming skills

see also
ACTIVEX APPLET, VBSCRIPT

jitter

fault on a monitor that manifests itself with very annoying, tiny movements of the characters displayed.

joystick

device that lets you control the movement of a cursor by tilting an upright rod. Usually used for games. In order to use a joystick, you'll need to fit a joystick controller card inside your PC. The first PCs had joystick ports fitted, but now it's common for the sound card to provide the joystick port. The port itself looks like a serial port connector with nine pins arranged within a D-shaped surround.

JPEG

standard that defines a way of storing graphic images in a compressed format in a file on disk; JPEG is a complex way of storing images in a compressed format so that they take up a fraction of the disk space of the uncompressed image.

see also
GIF, MPEG

jukebox

CD-ROM drive that can hold several CD-ROM discs and select the correct disc when required

justify

to align text so that both the left and right hand margins are flush and level. This is normally an option on your wordprocessor and is carried out automatically - the wordprocessor inserts tiny spaces between the words to make each margin level.

Kk

Kb or Kbyte
KILO BYTE

measure of the data capacity of a storage device that is equal to 1024 bytes. A more comprehensible way of imagining this is that in a document, each byte normally represents one character so one Kbyte is equal to 1024 characters. If you want to check the size of a document file (or anyother type of file) highlight the file name in Program Manager in Windows or type DIR at the DOS prompt - the size of the file is displayed after the file name. Rather confusingly, although one Kbyte is actually equal to 1024 bytes, many people use it to mean 1000 bytes. (The reason it's equal to 1024 is that this is equal to two to the power 10 - remember that computers only work in binary, base 2.)
see also
BINARY, MBYTE

Kbps
KILO BITS PER SECOND

measure of the amount of data that a device can transfer each second. A fast modem can transfer data at a rate of 33.6Kbps, wheras an ISDN adapter can transfer data at a rate of 64Kbps

kern
to adjust the space between pairs of characters so that they are printed closer together. For example, in a monospaced character set each character takes up the same width. This looks silly when you have an 'i' next to an 'l', so most character sets kern pairs of letters so that they look better when printed. Some sophisticated wordprocessors and DTP progrrams let you adjust the kerning between pairs of characters manually.

key
one of the individual buttons that make up your keyboard.

key combination/shortcut
combination of two or more keys that carry out a function when pressed at the same time. For example, the key combination Alt-S normally saves the file you are working on in any Windows program; Alt-F4 will exit the program you are using. To use these key combinations, hold down the Alt key (lower left, beside the spacebar) and press the second key.
see also
SHORTCUT

KHz
i) measure of the frequency of a sound that's equal to one thousand cycles per

second. The higher the number, the higher pitched the sound. Normal speech has a very limited frequency range - mostly between 300Hz and 2.4KHz, wheras music and other sounds can be heard at far higher and lower frequencies.

ii) You will also see KHz mentioned in the specification of a sound card. This can define two separate functions for the sound card: the first is the range of frequencies that the sound card can output and the second, and more usual use, is the frequency at which the sound card takes samples of a sound when recording it onto your disk. A sound card looks at the level of a sound (from a microphone) thousands of times each second and so builds up a picture of the sound. The more times it takes a sample, the more accurate the recording - and the number of times the sound card takes a sample per second is described in KHz. A good sound card would cope with 22KHz or 44KHz samples - 22,000 or 44,000 samples each second.

Kilostream

leased line connection supplied by British Telecom that provides data transfer rates of 64Kbit per second

see

LEASED LINE

LI

L2 cache
LEVEL TWO CACHE
high-speed cache memory that is fitted to the computer's motherboard, except on a
computer using the Pentium Pro processor where the memory is part of the
processor chip design

label
i) paper label stuck to the outside of a floppy disk on which you can write.
ii) text name assigned to a disk normally during formatting; this name appears at the
top of any DIR command or within the MyComputer window. To assign a new
name, use the LABEL command at the DOS prompt or, in Windows 95, highlight
the floppy disk icon and select its properties window and type in the new volume
name.

LAN
LOCAL AREA NETWORK
way of connecting several computers together within an office or building so that
you can exchange files or messages with another user on another computer that is
connected to the local area network. To setup a local area network, each PC needs a
network adapter fitted inside it and each then needs to be linked together with cable.
A wide area network is similar to a local area network, but links computers that are
miles apart - even those in different countries.

landscape document/orientation
layout of a piece of paper in which the longer edge is horizontal. This is useful if
you want to print out a wide spreadsheet or image. Documents and letters are
almost always printed with the paper in Portrait format - the long edge vertical. You
can change the orientation of the paper through Page Setup menu option of your
wordprocessor or spreadsheet program: if you select landscape format, the software
then tells Windows to rotate the text before printing it.
compare with
PORTRAIT

language
Windows 3.1 and 95 can both support different foreign languages. In most cases,
the foreign country has not only a different set of accented characters but also a
different keyboard layout. For example, the UK and USA use the QWERTY
keyboard layout (this describes the first keys on the top left hand row), whereas
France uses the AZERTY layout. If you want to use a different language for display
and printing you will have to change the language setup for both the font used to
support the accents and the keyboard layout for Windows. If you want to use some
Central European or Asian languages, you will need to buy new fonts for Windows

laptop

small portable computer that can be carried around; a laptop normally has a clam-shell construction with a fold-down lid that houses the screen, a keyboard (often slightly smaller than full-size) and a floppy disk and hard disk drive. An internal battery pack provides power for a few hours' use. Most new laptop computers now provide colour screens and as much computing power as a desktop but with the convenience of being portable.

laser printer

printer that produces very high quality text and graphics using a laser beam. The beam draws the characters as tiny dots - normally 300 or 600 dots per inch - onto a special drum; the drum then attracts a fine black powder (called toner) to these dots which is then trasferred onto a sheet of paper. The final stage is to heat the toner which melts it onto the paper forming a permanent printed image. A laser printer is more expensive than almost any other type of printer, but is generally faster and produces excellent print quality. The other types of printer include ink-jet printers that are slower and do not have such high quality print. There are also dot-matrix printers which are very noisy and have poor quality output, but are cheap and are the only type of printer that can handle multi-part invoices or other similar stationery.
see also
INK-JET, DOT-MATRIX

LaserJet™

brand name for a printer model produced by Hewlett Packard. The LaserJet has its own language called PCL that defined the way characters and graphics were printed on the page. This language has now become one of the two standards for sending data from a computer to a laser printer - the other language is called PostScript. Many laser printers are LaserJet compatible. This means that if you setup Windows so that it is configured to support an HP LaserJet printer, it will work with any LaserJet compatible printer.

latency

time taken for data to travel across a network or the internet from the sender to the destination

launch a program

to start a program. You can launch a program by double-clicking on its icon within Windows or by typing in the program name at the DOS prompt. Within Windows 95, you can launch a program by typing in the program name from the Start/Run menu command

layout

arrangement of the keys on a keyboard; different countries have different keyboard layouts - the UK and US have a standard QWERTY layout which refers to the order of the first keys on the top left-hand corner of the keyboard. Other countries have different key layouts according to their accents and local requirements. If you want to change the keyboard layout of your PC, you can plug in a different keyboard and congifure Windows to support this - using the Control Panel icon in Windows 3.1 or the Start/Settings menu option in Windows 95.

layout

way of using a sheet of paper; there are two basic layouts for any printed page: with the long edge horizontally which is called landscape or with the long edge vertically

which is called portrait.
see also
LANDSCAPE, PORTRAIT

LCD screen
LIQUID CRYSTAL DISPLAY SCREEN
technology used to create thin displays normally used in laptop or PDA computers; there are three types of LCD screen available: a monochrome screen, a colour DSTN screen and a colour TFT screen. The monochrome screen has a thin light source behind the screen that glows. This is the cheapest type of LCD screen available for laptop computers and provides a reasonably bright, clear display. The two colour LCD screens are now a standard feature of laptops. A DSTN screen is cheaper but does not have such good colour or contrast as a TFT screen.

leading
space between lines of text printed or displayed. It's usual to measure the leading between two lines of text in points - one point is equal to 1/72nd of an inch. If you increase the leading between lines of text, the lines are often clearer to read and nicer to look at.

leased line
permanent communications link between two sites; companies that want to setup their own internet server in-house would normally choose a leased line between their offices and the ISP (internet service provider). Two ISPs could use a fast leased line to connect to each other to transfer data. A leased line provides a permanent link with no call charges, unlike ISDN, however it is more expensive to install. If you are planning to install your own WWW server in your company, it will probably be cheaper to install a leased line than pay the call charges for an ISDN connection
see also
ISDN, KILOSTREAM

LED
LIGHT EMITTING DIODE
electronic component that emits light when an electrical current is passed through it. LEDs are often used as indicators on computers and printers or, in some cases, are used as the printing element in a printer instead of a laser
see also
LASER PRINTER

left-handed mouse
configuration of a mouse so that the function of the two buttons are reversed; if you are left-handed you can swap the functions of the two keys using the setup software supplied with the mouse or by using the Settings function of Windows 95

left-justify
to print or display a paragraph of text with the left-hand margin aligned and the right-hand margin of the text ragged.

level two cache
see
L2 CACHE

licence agreement

legal document that accompanies any commercial software product and defines how you can use the software and, importantly, how many people can use the software. Unless you buy a network version of a software product, the licence allows one person to use the software - copying the software is illegal. If you want several people to use the software or if you want to use the software on a network, then you need to buy a multi-user licence.

light emitting diode

see
LED

line

row of characters on a screen or printed on a page

line spacing

number of blank lines that are printed between each line of text. This dictionary, for example, is printed with a single line spacing. If you print with double-line spacing each line of text is separated by a blank line.

compare with
LEADING

linked object

one piece of data that is referred to in another file or application. For example, if you open a spreadsheet program and a wordprocessor in two adjacent windows and drag the spreadsheet data into your document, Windows actually creates a link between the two files. The spreadsheet file is called an object and is linked into the document in your wordprocessor.

see also
OLE

linking information

(in Windows) feature that allows you to insert data from one application into a another application using its OLE function. For example, you can include a spreadsheet inside a document, which is then automatically updated whenever the spreadsheet changes.

see also
OLE

list box

number of items or options displayed in a list; for a long list you can scroll up and down through the list using a scroll bar

listserv *or* listserver

server on the internet that sends a newsletter or articles to a list of registered users; there are tens of thousands of listservers on the internet that cover all sorts of subjects, from computing to Spanish, teaching to travelling. If you want to keep up to date with a specialist subject, join the related listserver. Any user can submit information that might be useful to the other users and this information is sent automatically by email to all registered users on the list. Anyone can become a member of a list, see sites such as www.liszt.com that catalogues all the lists available. The management of a listserver is normally carried out by a majordomo: if you want to subscribe to a list so that you start receiving information, send a

message to the majordomo at the list
see also
AUTOMATIC MAILING LIST, MAJORDOMO

Live3D™
see
VRML

local
i) (hardware device) that is attached to your computer.
ii) (software) an application that is running on your computer.

local area network (LAN)
way of connecting several computers together within an office or building so that you can exchange files or messages with another user on another computer that is connected to the local area network. To setup a local area network, each PC needs a network adapter fitted inside it and each then needs to be linked together with cable. A wide area network is similar to a local area network, but links computers that are miles apart - even those in different countries.

local bus
expansion bus within a PC that allows data to travel around the computer very fast. Normally, you would use the local bus to connect a graphics adapter to your computer to get the best possible performance when displaying images.
see
PCI, VL-BUS

LocalTalk™
networking standard used by Apple Macintosh computers to connect Apple computers together in a local area network. If you want to connect your PC to a Mac network, you need to get a LocalTalk network adapter and software for your PC.

log on
command that tells the network you want to use the network resources. Normally, you need to enter your user name and password which is then verified by the network software before allowing you to access the resouces.

log off
to stop using a network and work individually. Your computer is still physically connected to the network, but you have told the network software that you do not want to use the network features or resources. Log off can apply either to a local area network or to an online system, such as CompuServe or MSN. In the case of the latter two, you log off and disconnect by hanging up the phone line to the online service.

logic
i) Boolean algebraic operations that determine the outcome of binary numbers based on conditions.
ii) term sometimes used to describe low-level programming commands
see also
BOOLEAN

login
to enter your user name and password that allows the computer to check that you

are an authorised user of the computer or network and permit you to use the resources

login script

series of instructions that are automatically run when you log into a network. For example, if you log into your office network in the morning by typing your name and password, the login script might remind you of important information or just display 'good morning'.

logoff

steps that you carry out to stop using a computer or network, usually a single command like 'bye' or 'shutdown'

long filename

feature of Windows 95 that lets you give files a long name (up to 254 characters long). Before Windows 95 was released, file names were limited to a maximum of just eight characters. For example, before your letter would be called 'MEMO27.DOC' now you can call it 'memo to Simon about project delta'. If you try and access files that have a long filename within an older version of MS-DOS that does not support this feature, then the filenames are shortened with a ~ symbol but can still be accessed correctly

low memory

memory locations from zero up to 640Kb.

see also
HIGH MEMORY, EXPANDED MEMORY

low-power standby

energy saving feature of laptop computers and many monitors connected to a desktop. If you do not use the computer for a few minutes, it will shut down some parts of the electronics - normally the hard disk drive and the screen or monitor. When you start typing or move the mouse, the computer switches these parts back on to normal power levels.

see also
ENERGY STAR

LPT

LINE PRINTER
acronym that refers to the main parallel printer port on a PC
compare with
COM

Mm

M
MEGA-

prefix meaning an amount equal to 2^{20} or 1,048,576

m
MILLI-

prefix meaning an amount equal to one thousandth

Macintosh™
personal computer developed by Apple; the Macintosh uses the Motorola 68000 series of processor and is not compatible with the IBM PC. The Macintosh was one of the first computers to provide a graphical user interface (called the System) that provides an easy-to-use front-end for the computer.

macro
series of commands or operations that are named and can be run at any time. For example, if you always carry out a series of operations on your text to turn it into a monthly report (perhaps, changing the font, adding a table, searching and replacing one character for another), then you could record a macro to do all these functions automatically. Almost all wordprocessor and spreadsheet programs can record and playback macros and Microsoft has taken this one step further by including the VBA (Visual Basic for Applications) programming language into its main applications such as Word and Excel to allow you to create complex macros

magnetic storage
method of storing information as magnetic changes on a sensitive tape or disk, such as a floppy disk or hard disk
compare with
CD-ROM, RAM

magneto-optical recording
type of disc that stores data on an optical disc. It is similar to a CD-ROM, but the difference is that you can write to and erase data from an MOR disc many times. A magneto-optical disc can store over 600Mb of data.

mail application programming interface
see
MAPI

mailbox
storage location that contains a user's mail messages; if you are using electronic mail sent via the internet, the mailbox will be on a mail server computer at the ISP. To read your mail messages, you need email software that can communicate with

the mail server computer to send the messages

see also
POP3, SMTP

mail merge

to automatically include the address details from a database into a standard (or form) letter. For example, if you want to tell all your customers that your prices of goods are increasing, write one standard form letter and then include the name and address fields from your customer database. Almost all wordprocessor programs let you carry out a mail merge with an external database.

mail server

computer that stores incoming mail and sends it to the correct user and stores outgoing mail and transfers it to the correct destination server on the internet

mail-enabled application

application from which it is possible to send mail without specifically calling up your email package. Lotus is mail-enabling new releases of its Windows packages to automatically call up cc:Mail; WinMail supplies macros to mail-enable standard applications.

mail

see
ELECTRONIC MAIL

majordomo

see
LISTSERV

management information services

see
MIS

MAPI

MAIL APPLICATION PROGRAMMING INTERFACE
set of standards (developed by Microsoft) that defines how electronic mail is sent and delivered

mapping

linking a directory path to a local drive letter, enabling a user to log directly onto a server's network drive without having to select volumes, directories and files individually.

mapping (a drive or printer)

connecting a disk drive or a printer that is connected to another computer on a network. To access the files stored on a disk drive of another computer you have to assign it a drive letter - this process is called mapping a network drive. Your PC probably has a floppy disk drive (called A:) and a hard disk drive (called C:). You could map E: to point to a disk drive that is actually located on another computer on the network. To map a drive or printer is far easier than the explanation! Windows 95 and other network software lets you drag and drop the icon of another user's computer onto your own to create the mapping automatically.

margins
blank spaces at the top, bottom, left and right of a printed page.

maths coprocessor
processor component that is designed to help the main processor chip by carrying out calculations with floating point numbers, speeding up mathematical operations
see also
COPROCESSOR

maximise
command that increases the size of a window (in Windows) so that it fills the entire screen. In Windows 3.x you can maximise any window by clicking on the Maximise button - the up arrow at the very top right-hand corner of the window. In Windows 95, click on the middle of the three buttons in the top right-hand corner of the window

Mb or Mbyte
MEGABYTE
measure of the data capacity of a storage device that is equal to 1,048,576 bytes (which is equal to two raised to the power of 20). Megabytes are used to measure the storage capacity of hard disk drives or main memory (RAM).
see also
BINARY, KBYTE

MCA
MICRO CHANNEL ARCHITECTURE
design of an expansion bus connector inside the PS/2 range of IBM computers. The MCA bus provides 32-bit data transfer, is fast, but requires a special type of adapter that is more expensive than standard adapters.
see also
EISA, EXPANSION BUS, LOCAL BUS

MCI
MEDIA CONTROL INTERFACE
commands that allow any program control multimedia, such as a sound card or video clip. You never see raw MCI commands, but you might see them referenced - the Media Player and Sound Recorded applets within Windows work by sending out MCI commands.

MDRAM
MULTIBANK DYNAMIC RANDOM ACCESS MEMORY
high performance memory normally used in video adapter cards to provide fast graphic display

media
i) something that stores or carries information - it's a rather vague term, but in computing it generally refers to diskettes or CD-ROM discs.
ii) information that is used within a multimedia presentation and can be sound, graphics, or video.

media control interface
see
MCI

Media Player™

utility program supplied free with Windows that allows you to control installed multimedia hardware including video disc or audio CDs or playback multimedia files including sound, animation and video files. To run this program, select Start/Programs/Accessories/Multimedia from the Windows 95 toolbar

meg

slang term for a megabyte.

mega-

prefix meaing 2^{20} or 1,048,576

megabyte

see
MB

megaflop

MILLION FLOATING POINT

measure of the speed of a processor calculated as the number of mathematical calculations it can carry out per second

megahertz

see
MHZ

Memmaker™

software utility supplied with some versions of Microsoft MS-DOS and used to automatically configure the computer's memory settings to provide optimum performance

memory

device that can store information, but generally used to refer to electronic components that can store data and are used to provide the RAM in your computer that's used to run the software. Electronic memory chips only 'remember' data for as long as electricity is supplied. This is not the same as disk storage which is long-term data storage on magnetic media.
see also
EPROM, DRAM, FLASH RAM, RAM, ROM

memory chip

electronic component that stores binary data
see also
EPROM, DRAM, FLASH RAM, RAM, ROM

memory expansion

to add more electronic memory chips to your computer; your PC needs memory to run software programs and Windows needs as much memory as possible - 8Mb of RAM is a reasonable quantity.

memory management unit

see
MMU

menu

list of options available in a program
see also
DROP-DOWN, PULL-DOWN

menu bar

line of options available that run along the top of a window; when one of the words in the menu bar is selected, a further list of options is displayed beneath the word (this is called a drop-down menu). For example, almost all Windows programs have a menu bar that starts with the word 'File'. If you select the word File, it displays a list of menu options that include Open, Save and Exit.

menu driven

software that is operated by selecting options from menus rather than by typing in a command word
compare with
COMMAND LINE

menu item

single choice displayed in a menu

menu shortcuts

key combination of two or more keys that are the same are selecting a menu option. For example, if you want to save the document you are working on in your wordprocessor, you can either choose the File menu and pick Save from the list or press Ctrl-S which is the standard menu shortcut.
see also
HOTKEY, SHORTCUT

message box

small window that is displayed on screen to warn you of an event or condition or error. For example, if you try and save a document with the same name as an existing file, a message box pops up to ask if you want to change the filename or replace the existing file with the new one.

meter - power supply

utility within Windows 95 displayed as an icon in the bottom right-hand corner of the status bar that indicates how much power is left in your laptop's battery and whether your laptop is running from a battery or mains electricty power.

MFM

MODIFIED FREQUENCY MODULATION
system of recording data onto a magnetic hard disk
compare with
RLL

MHS

MESSAGE HANDLING SERVICE
store-and-forward message transfer mechanism used mainly by Novell; this system allows electronic mail messages to be sent between users on a network or to users on remote networks
compare with
MAPI, VIM

MHz
MEGAHERTZ

measure of the frequency of a timing signal that's equal to one million cycles per second. The higher the number, the faster the clock that's generating the timing signal. This normally refers to the main clock that sets the timing signal for the processor chip in your PC. The faster the timing signal, the faster the processor will run and so the faster your software will run; current high-performance processors use a clock that has a frequency of 200MHz - the original PC used a clock with a frequency of just 4.77MHz

micro-
(prefix) means one millionth

micro
outdated term that refers to a personal computer

Micro Channel Architecture™
MCA

design of an expansion bus connector inside the PS/2 range of IBM computers. The MCA bus provides 32-bit data transfer, is fast, but requires a special type of adapter that is more expensive than standard adapters.
see also
EISA, ISA

microfloppy
name for the 3.5-inch floppy disk

microphone
device that converts sound waves into electrical signals. In order to record speech or sound on your PC you need a sound card that can convert and store electrical signals and a microphone that converts sound to electrical signals.

microprocessor
see
CPU

Microsoft™
software publisher that created Windows, MS-DOS, Word, Excel and many other applications. It dominates the software world for both the PC and Macintosh.

Microsoft Exchange™
program included with Windows 95 that coordinates the electronic mail, fax and network messages you send and receive on your PC. You need to install the Exchange software when you install Windows 95 on your PC and you'll see the InBox icon of Exchange appear on your Desktop.

Microsoft Exchange Server™
program that runs on a server under Microsoft Windows NT and provides sophisticated groupware functions using the Exchange client software supplied with Windows 95

Microsoft Fax™
series of programs supplied with Windows 3.1 and 95 that let you send and receive fax transmissions from your PC. The Fax software also lets you create coversheets

for the fax transmissions.

Microsoft internet Explorer™
Web brower developed by Microsoft, currently available free, that allows a user to view Web pages; supports many features including ActiveX applets
see also
NETSCAPE

Microsoft Network™ (MSN)
online service that was launched by Microsoft to provide information, weather, database links to the internet and electronic mail especially for Windows 95 users. The software required to access MSN is built-into Windows 95.

Microsoft Windows™
operating system developed by Microsoft designed to make PCs easier to use; Windows is a GUI (pronounced gooeey) - a graphical user interface. It lets you control the computer using a mouse and represents files and folders as icons on screen. Before Windows was developed, PC users had to type commands into MS-DOS. The current version is Windows 95 that includes features to allow access to the internet, allow users to send and receive fax and electronic mail messages
see also
GUI, WINDOWS

MIDI
MUSICAL INTRUMENT DIGITAL INTERFACE
special interface that lets your computer control musical intruments, such as a synthesizer, keyboard or drum machine. To create a MIDI setup you need a MIDI interface for your PC - which is often part of a sound card - and a cable that runs to your musical instrument.

MIDI file
file stored on your PC that contains musical notes and sound information that can be sent via a MIDI interface card to a musical instrument. MIDI files can also contain information that describes the type of sound played as well as the note - for example, to inform the synthesizer to sound like a piano or trumpet.

MIDI Mapper
program that's supplied with Windows 3.1x and that allows experienced MIDI users to change the way in which musical notes are sent to each instrument that's connected to the PC. For example, you could use the MIDI Mapper to re-direct all the notes meant for the drum machine to the electronic piano.

milli- (m)
prefix meaning one thousandth

million instructions per second
see
MIPS

MIME
MULTIPURPOSE INTERNET MAIL EXTENSIONS
standard that defines a way of sending files using electronic mail software. MIME allows a user to send files over the internet to another user without having to carry out any other encoding or conversion actions. MIME was developed to get around a

problem of many electronic mail systems that could only transmit text which is stored in a 7-bit data format; programs, multimedia, graphics and other files are stored using an 8-bit data format. Before MIME was developed, you would have to first encode the file then send it as a text mail message; the recipient would then have to decode the text file back to its original state

minimise

to shrink an application window down to an icon so that the application is still running in the background, but is not the active window. To do this, select the down-arrow button in the top right-hand corner of the window (or the first of the three buttons in a Windows 95 window). Minimising an application allows you to run several applications at the same time, minimising the ones you're not using. In Windows 3.1x the minimised applications appear as an icon in the bottom left hand corner of the screen. To go back to the application, double-click on the minimised icon. In Windows 95, the application shrinks down to an icon on the status bar; you can switch back to the application with a single click on the icon.

MIPS

MILLION INSTRUCTIONS PER SECOND
measure of processor speed that defines the number of instructions it can carry out per second
compare with
MEGAFLOPS

mirroring

method of improving fault tolerance in a network. In a mirrored disk system, two separate hard disks are connected to the same controller. The same data is duplicated on the two drives by one controller. This offers a cheaper, but less secure, fault tolerance than disk duplexing.

MIS

MANAGEMENT INFORMATION SERVICES
department in a large company that runs the computer systems

MMU

MEMORY MANAGEMENT UNIT
electronic component in a computer that manages the way in which data is stored in different RAM chips

MMX

MULTIMEDIA EXTENSIONS
processor chip that includes components that are used to improve the performance when dealing with multimedia and communications; typically, these improvements allow the processor to manage many different data sources at the same time, improving the way it can handle image processing, video, speech

mnemonic

key sequence that is a shortcut to a menu option or function in an application. For example, pressing the Alt and F4 (written Alt-F4) keys at the same time will exit an application. Similarly, Ctrl and S (Ctrl-S) will save your current document in Microsoft applications.

MNP

set of error-control standards developed by Microcom Inc. and adopted into the

CCITT V.42 standard. MNP allows a modem or communications program to detect transmission errors and request a resend.

MNP 2-4
error-correcting communications protocol developed by Microcom Inc. and adopted into the CCITT V.42 standard. MNP allows a modem or communications program to detect transmission errors and request a resend.

MNP 5
communications standard that provides data compression, providing up to 2-to-1 compression (though averaging less).

MNP 10
error correcting communications protocol that can transfer data accurately even over poor-quality telephone connections. It adjusts rapidly to changing line conditions to get the best throughput. MNP 10 has been adopted for cellular modems.

modal
(in Windows) window that's displayed and that doesn't allow you to do anything outside it. For example, dialog boxes are normally modal windows - you have to reply to the dialog box before you can continue with the application.

modem
device that converts electronic signals from your computer into sound signals that can be transmitted over a telephone line. To receive information, the modem works in reverse and converts the sound signals back into digital electronic signals. Modems are used to connect your computer to the internet (using an ISP) or to an on-line service, such as CompuServe. Some modems are internal - you have to open your PC and fit the modem into a free expansion slot. Most modems are external and plug into the serial port of your computer. Current modems can transfer data at 33,600 bits per second, which is roughly equivalent to one and a half pages of A4 text every second. If you are shopping for a modem, make sure it has error detection and correction functions (see entries for V.42 and V.42bis). Most modems now also offer fax features that allows you to send and receive text and images to other fax machines. Lastly, many newer modems provide voice-mail features that allow your computer to work as a sophisticated answering machine
see also
ISP, TELEPHONY, V42

moderated list
mailing list in which someone reads all the material that has been submitted before it is distributed to the users on the list

modified frequency modulation
see
MFM

monitor
device that displays the text and graphics from your computer. It looks and works rather like a TV set. Images are displayed as tiny dots on the screen (the smaller and closer the dots, the sharper the image). If you do a lot of design or DTP, you might consider a screen that's bigger than the usual 15-inch (which is normally measured

across the longest diagonal).
see also
MULTISYNC MONITOR.

monochrome monitor
monitor that can only display black, white and grey text and images.

monospaced font
font in which each character has the same width, making it easy to align tables and columns. In Windows, the monospaced font is called Courier.

morphing
special effect used in multimedia and games in which one image gradually turns into another. For example, a tiger might gradually turn into a bucket over a few seconds.

motherboard
main circuit board within your computer. If you open your PC (with the mains electricity unplugged), you'll see the motherboard at the bottom of the case. It's normally varnished green to protect the tiny connections and has the main electronic components and connectors soldered onto it.

Motorola
company that designs and makes the 68000 range of processors that are used in Macintosh and Atari computers. Its latest processor is the PowerPC chip that is used in workstations and Apple Macintosh computers
see also
INTEL

mouse
small, hand-held device that's moved on a flat surface to control the position of a pointer on screen. A mouse normally has two buttons. In Windows, the left-hand button selects text or starts an application. The right-hand button displays options for the item. If you want to change a file so that it can only be read, and not written to, move the pointer to the file name (in Windows 95 Explorer) and select the file with a single click on the left-hand button. Now click once on the right-hand button to display the properties for this file.

mouse acceleration
feature of some mouse driver software that will move the mouse pointer at different speeds according to the speed (not the distance) at which you move the mouse. For example, if you move the mouse slowly, the pointer will move slowly to allow you to carry out delicate tasks; if you move the mouse suddenly, the pointer will accelerate and move much further and faster

mouse-driven
software that is controlled using a mouse rather than by typing in commands.

mouse driver
special software that converts the movement of a mouse into position signals that inform Windows of the new position of the pointer on screen.

mouse pointer
(in Windows) small arrow that's displayed on screen and moves as you move the

mouse. The pointer is used to select and start applications. It can also change shape to an 'I' beam pointer.

mouse sensitivity
ratio of how far the pointer moves on screen in relation to the distance you move the mouse - high mouse sensitivity means that a small movement of the mouse results in a small movement of the pointer

mouse tracking
inverse of mouse sensitivity: high mouse tracking means that a small movement of the mouse results in in a large movement of the pointer, useful if you want to move around the screen quickly, but do not want to do detailed work

movie file
file stored on disk that contains a series of images that make up an animation or video clip.

moving pictures expert group
see
MPEG

MPC
MULTIMEDIA PC
set of minimum requirements for a PC that will allow it to run most multimedia software. Generally refers to PCs that have 4Mb or more of RAM, a 486SX processor or better, at least a 160Mb hard disk, a CD-ROM XA drive, 16-bit sound card and MIDI port.

MPEG
MOVING PICTURES EXPERT GROUP
group of developers that have defined a series of standards to improve audio and video quality but at the same time increase data compression so that the video sequence takes less disk space but retains a high quality image
see also
JPEG

ms
MILLISECOND
one thousandth of a second, often used to measure the time taken for hard disk access
see also
ACCESS TIME

MS-DOS
MICROSOFT DOS
operating system software developed by Micrsoft that controls and coordinates the basic functions of your computer. If you are running Windows 95, the functions of MS-DOS have been integrated into Windows. If you are using Windows 3.1x or do not have Windows, then you are relying on MS-DOS (or a similar product from IBM called PC-DOS) to control the computer.
see also
OPERATING SYSTEM

MSN
see
MICROSOFT NETWORK

MTBF
MEAN TIME BETWEEN FAILURES
specification for new electronic equipment, such as a new hard disk, that specifies the number of hours (often tens of thousands) for which the equipment can be used before it is expected to go wrong.

multibank dynamic random access memory
see
MDRAM

multi-part stationery
stationery that has several sheets laid together that produce copies without carbon paper. Don't forget that only impact printers, such as dot-matrix or daisy-wheel printers, will print correctly with multi-part stationery.

multifrequency monitor
see
MULTISYNC MONITOR

multimedia
combination of text, images, video, sound and animation within an application.
see also
MPC

multimedia extensions
see
MMX

multimedia-ready
PC that has all the extra equipment requirement to run most multimedia software. Normally, this means that it runs the Microsoft Windows operating system, is fitted with a CD-ROM drive, large hard disk, 8Mb of RAM and a sound card with speakers.

multipurpose internet mail extensions
see
MIME

multiscan monitor
see
MULTISYNC MONITOR

multisession compatible
CD-ROM drive that can read PhotoCD discs or other discs that have been created in several goes. For example, if you save one photograph onto a PhotoCD disc on Monday and another two on Tuesday, you have created a multisession disc. When buying a CD-ROM drive, make sure that it is multisession-compatible.

multisync monitor
monitor that can be plugged into different types of computer and display different

graphic resolutions. For example, if you have a normal desktop PC with S-VGA graphics (at a resolution of 800x600 pixels) and want to plug this monitor into your laptop computer, which uses an older EGA standard, the monitor will only display the images if it is multi-scan and can automatically switch between resolutions.

multitasking

ability of Windows to run several programs at once. For example, under Windows you can sort a database address list while typing in a letter. The trick is that Windows actually switches repeatedly and very rapidly between the tasks, giving you the impression that they are running in parallel.

music chip

special electronic component on a sound card that creates the sounds which are then amplified and played back through speakers; some music chips create sounds from pre-recorded samples, others generate each sound according to your music software

musical instrument digital interface

see
MIDI

My Computer

icon that is normally in the upper left-hand corner of the screen on a computer running Windows 95 and contains an overview of your PC. If you double-click on this icon, you'll see all the peripherals that are connected to your PC including hard disk, floppy disk, CD-ROM and any printers

see also
DESKTOP

Nn

n
NANO-
prefix that means one billionth, often used to indicate the speed or access time of memory chips

name
description given to a file, folder, printer or computer on a network. If you want to change the name of folder in Windows 95, move the pointer over the name and click once. Wait a couple of seconds and you'll be able to type in a new name.

name server
computer on the internet that provides a domain name service to any other computer
see
DNS

naming services
method of assigning each user or node or computer on a network a unique name that allows other users to access shared resources even over a wide area network.

nano-
see
N

nanosecond
see
NS

National Center for Supercomputing Applications (NCSA)
organisation that helped define and create the world wide web with its Mosaic Web browser

NC
see
NETWORK COMPUTER

near-letter quality
NLQ
printer that is almost as good as a traditional typewriter. This now covers just about all printers except some cheap or very fast dot-matrix printers that still look 'dotty'.

nerd
(slang term for a) person who is obsessed with computers and rarely talks or thinks

about anything that is not technologically exciting
see also
GEEK

NetBIOS
NETWORK BASIC INPUT/OUTPUT SYSTEM
low level software interface that lets applications talk to network hardware. If a
network is NetBIOS compatible, it will respond in the same way to the set of
NetBIOS commands, accessed from DOS by the 5Ch interrupt. NetBIOS was the de
facto standard, thanks to a lack of international standards, but its limitations and age
now make it near redundant.

Netscape Navigator™
one of the most popular WWW browsers that still dominates the marketplace;
includes many features including a news reader, and supports Java applets (to read
details of the newest developments, look at www.netscape.com WWW site)
see also
BROWSER, HTML, INTERNET EXPLORER, JAVA

NetView™
network management architecture developed by IBM. Information about the way
the network and nodes are working is sent to a central computer that provides
reports that help a network manager spot any warning signs

NetWare™
network operating system, developed by Novell, that dominates the local area
networking market; one central server computer runs the NetWare software and
other workstations connect to this server to share files, resources and printers
see also
NETWORK OPERATING SYSTEM

network
way of connecting several computers and printers together so that they can
exchange information. To set up a network, each PC needs a network adapter and a
cable that forms the connection between each; there are two basic types of network:
a peer-to-peer network in which each computer can share its own files with other
computers, or a server-based network which has a main dedicated computer to
which all the other computers are connected
see also
NETWORK NEIGHBORHOOD, PEER-TO-PEER, SERVER

network adapter
board that plugs into an expansion socket inside your PC and converts data into
electrical signals that are then transmitted over an electrical cable to other
computers on a network; if you want to link three computers together so that they
can each share files and resources, you have to fit a network adapter into each
computer and link each with cable

network computer (NC)
new type of computer that, it is predicted, will change the way computers are used.
The network computer is designed to run Java programs and access information
using a web browser. It has a small desktop box that does not have a floppy disk
drive, instead it downloads any software it requires from a central server. Network
computers are simpler and cheaper than current PCs and Macintosh computers, and

are designed to be easier to manage in a large company.

network drive
disk drive that you can access, but that is physically located on another PC on the network. To Windows, it appears to be just another disk drive - although its icon shows a tiny cable running beneath it. To view the network drives that are currently mapped to your computer, use the Network Neighborhood utility

network interface card (NIC)
see
NETWORK ADAPTER

Network Neighborhood
utility that is part of Windows 95 that allows you to view and manage connections to your computer; if Windows 95 detects that you are connected to another computer, it will display the Network Neighborhood icon on your Desktop. This utility shows the other computers linked into the network and allows you to share the files stored on their disk drives or use a network drive or printer.

network operating system (NOS)
software that carries out all the functions required to support a network; the network operating system software normally runs on a dedicated server computer and each user's computer is linked to the server. The NOS manages the way in which files and printers are shared and ensures that unauthorised users cannot access the resources. The two main network operating systems used with PCs are Novell NetWare and Microsoft Windows NT/AS. Peer-to-peer networks do not use a dedicated server running network operating system software, instead each computer runs network software
see also
PEER TO PEER

network printer
printer connected to a computer that is also connected to a network, allowing you to use the printer as if it were connected directly to your PC.

network server
dedicated computer that runs network operating system software; the network server forms the centre of the network, with all the other computers connected to the server. Each computer can store files on the server's disk drive, or can print to a printer connected to the server. Small networks are often setup as a peer-to-peer network in which each computer can share files with others on the network. Large networks use a main network server that can be easily managed centrally

newsgroup
feature of the internet that provides free-for-all discussion forums; newsgroups are one area within what's often called Usenet - a newsgroup lets anyone discuss a particular topic and there are over 15,000 different newsgroups that cover just about every subject available. Newsgroups are one of the most active parts of the internet: you can read messages from other users, comment on them or submit your own message. To view newsgroups you need a connection to the internet, either via an ISP or an on-line service such as CompuServe; you will also need special news reader software that lets you view the newsgroups together with the articles in each group. The Netscape Navigator Web browser provides these functions as part of the software and Microsoft provides utilities to view newsgroups for its internet

Explorer software
see also
ALT, BIZ, COMP, USENET

news reader
software that allows a user to view the list of newsgroups and read the articles
posted in each group or submit a new article

NIC
see
NETWORK INTERFACE CARD

NiCad
NICKEL-CADMIUM

type of rechargeable battery used in laptops but now superseded by the NiMH
battery. NiCad batteries unfortunately have one problem called 'memory' which
gradually reduces their ability to retain charge; to remove the memory you should
condition a battery by running it right down so that it has no charge, before re-
charging it

NiMH
NICKEL METAL HYDRIDE

type of rechargeable battery now used in laptops; has better charge-carrying ability
than a NiCad battery, is quicker to charge and does not suffer from 'memory'

NLQ
see
NEAR LETTER QUALITY

node
device that is connected to a network, such as a computer or printer

noise
unwanted random signal that sounds like hissing on a recorded sound.

non-interlaced
method of building up an image on a display using one pass over the entire screen
compare with
INTERLACED

nonmaskable interrupt
electronic signal from a device that cannot be ignored by the processor, normally
generated by an important device, such as a reset button

nonvolatile
memory that can retain information even when electrical power is not supplied to
the device; a magnetic disk is nonvolatile, wheras a RAM chip is a volatile memory

notebook computer
small portable computer that's normally designed as a folding clam-shell with a
hinge at one edge, a flat LCD screen and a small keyboard. Notebook computers are
normally lighter than laptops and have a smaller screen and keyboard.

ns
NANOSECOND
one billionth of a second, used to measure the access speed of RAM memory

NT
see
WINDOWS NT

null modem cable
special cable that lets you link together two computers via their serial ports so that they can exchange files.

NumLock key
key on the top-left of the numeric keypad that switches the keypad between cursor control actions and number entry

NVRAM
NON-VOLATILE RANDOM ACCESS MEMORY
memory that can permanently retain information

Oo

o/p
see
OUTPUT

object
something that exists within an computer's user interface or operating system; for example, a folder is an object; a section of text, graphics, part of spreadsheet, even, in some cases, users and printers are objects.

object linking and embedding (OLE)
system within Windows that allows information created and formatted in one application to be used directly within another, different application; for example, you can create a spreadsheet using Excel, then switch to a wordprocessor and insert the spreadsheet file into the document. To insert objects, select the Edit/Paste Special menu command and you'll see a list of the types of object that you can include. Windows currently uses the OLE2 specification that allows greater flexibility and power when linking objects between applications

object-oriented
method of creating software so that each part of the program is a separate object that works independently and can respond and react to other objects or events that occur in the system; for example, under Microsoft Windows, a window is an object, each menu option is an object. When you select a menu option, this sends a message to the program code that controls the menu object, which can then respond correctly

Object Packager
utility included with Windows 3.x that lets you convert data from an application that does not support OLE so that it can be used as an OLE object in another application; this is redundant in Windows 95 since all programs for this platform support OLE

OCR
OPTICAL CHARACTER RECOGNITION
software application that can covert bitmap text stored in an image file (i.e. the result of scanning in a page of text) into characters that can be edited with a wordprocessor.

odd parity
way of transmitting data over a communications link that provides a very basic way of checking for transmission errors; the communications software counts how many '1's there are in each block of data it will transmit and sets an extra check bit to ensure that there is an odd number of '1's in the data. If you are setting up your

communications software to dial into a bulletin board system or online service, you will need to know whether the service requires even or odd parity. Most services expect you to use even parity - except CompuServe which often uses odd parity. Communications software packages like HyperTerminal in Windows 95 let you set the parity to either even or odd

see also
EVEN PARITY, PARITY

OEM
ORIGINAL EQUIPMENT MANUFACTURER
company that produces equipment (e.g. a computer) using basic parts made by other companies

offline
printer that is switched on, but is not ready to accept data. For example, if your laser printer runs out of paper, it normally automatically switches to offline mode until you insert more paper; it then switches back to online mode and continues printing. To stop printing at any time, press the online button to switch offline.

OK button
(in Windows) button displayed on screen with the label 'OK'. If you click on this button, you accept the choice or options.

OLE
see
OBJECT LINKING AND EMBEDDING

online
i) modem that is connected to another modem via a telphone line and is currently transferring information.
ii) a printer that is ready and waiting to print

online help
help screen displayed about a particular function of a program

open
i) to access a file and read its contents using an application. Most Windows applications will read a file via the File/Open menu option.
ii) to look inside a folder to view the list of files or sub-folders stored within it - open a folder with a double-click

open file
file that is currently being read from or written to by an application or another user on a network

operating system
software that controls and coordinates the actions of the different parts of your computer. In older computers, the operating system is called MS-DOS. In new PCs, Windows 95 is the operating system that manages the screen, keyboard, disks and printers.

operator
symbol that defines a mathematical action, for example 'x' is the multiplication operator.

optical character recognition
see
OCR

optical disc
flat, plastic disc that can store data in the form of tiny holes or bubbles created in a central layer using a laser. Some optical discs can be written to several times, others, like a CD-ROM, are manufactured with the data in place and cannot have data written onto them.

optical mouse
older-style mouse that uses a light sensor beneath the mouse to detect movement. The mouse is moved over a special mouse mat which has tiny location dots printed onto it.

OR
Boolean function that is often used in searches to ask the search engine to find text that contains any of the search words; for example, if you enter 'dog OR cat' the results will include all documents that contain the words dog or cat
see also
AND, BOOLEAN

orientation
way in which a piece of paper is held; for example, portrait orientation is with the longer edge vertical; landscape orientation is with the longer edge horizontal.
see also
LANDSCAPE, PORTRAIT

origin
start of a counter or ruler; if you are using a paint or drawing program, the positions are normally measured from the origin which is in the top left hand corner of the work.

original
artwork or photograph that has been scanned or copied.

original equipment manufacturer
see
OEM

orphan
first line of a paragraph printed at the bottom of a column, with the rest of the paragraph printed at the top of the next column.

OS
see
OPERATING SYSTEM

OS/2
operating system developed by IBM that provides a powerful, multitasking graphical environment; OS/2 is currently in a version called Warp that looks similar to Microsoft Windows. Currently, applications written for OS/2 will not run under Windows, however Windows applications can run under OS/2 Warp

outline font

font that is described by geometric shapes and lines, which can be scaled to any size without losing sharpness. Windows includes TrueType fonts that are outline fonts and can be printed in any size.

compare with
BITMAP FONTS

outliner

software application that lets you organize your thoughts, ideas and their structure. Each headword can have many sub-sections beneath it - these too can have sub-sections or bullet points and you can view all the sections or just the headwords.

output

anything that is produced by your PC - for example, a printout or sound.

Overdrive

processor chip that is used as a more powerful replacement for a conventional Intel 80486 processor

overlay

(i) strip of paper that is placed above the function keys on the keyboard to describe their function in a particular application.

ii) electronic device that will convert a video camera or TV signal so that it can be displayed in a window on screen

overlay card

see
VIDEO GRAPHICS CARD

Pp

p
PICO-
one trillionth

packet
basic unit of data sent over the network during intercommunication. A packet includes the address of the sending and receiving stations, error control information and check procedures, and, finally, the information itself.

packet switching
method of sending a series of packets of information over a network in which each packet does not necessarily have to travel via the same route from originator to destination; the software sending the information decides the route over the network for each packet and the receiving software re-assembles the packets in the correct order

page
i) block of memory used in a memory management scheme; data can be stored in individual pages of memory and moved to and from the hard disk as and when required, the memory management software uses pages of memory to get around the 640Kb limit of MS-DOS.

ii) one section of a document.

iii) one screen of information

see also
EXPANDED MEMORY, VIRTUAL MEMORY

page break
point at which one page of text stops and the next starts. In Word, you can insert the special character that stops one page by pressing Ctrl-Enter.

page description language (PDL)
series of codes and keywords that describe to a printer where and how to print text and graphics. When you print from a wordprocessor, Windows normally generates a complex series of page description language codes that are then sent to the printer

see also
PCL

page down key (PgDn)
key that moves down one page in a wordprocessor

page preview
function within a wordprocessor or other application that lets you view the way the printed page, text, graphics and margins will look before they are printed.

page printer

printer that prints a page in one go; generally refers to a laser printer; an ink-jet or dot-matrix printer creates a printed page one line at a time and they are called line printers.

page setup

options within an application that let you define the margins, paper orientation and paper size for the document.

page up key (PgUp)

key that moves up one page in a wordprocessor

pages per minute (ppm)

number of standard A4 text pages that a printer can print out each minute. A standard laser printer can print between 6-12 ppm, whereas a slower and cheaper ink-jet might manage 2-3ppm.

paint program

program that lets you draw, cut, paste and edit a bitmap image. There are normally a series of tools that include a spray-can effect, and tools to draw circles, boxes and lines. Sophisticated paint programs can be used to edit scanned photographs and to adjust colours and remove any hair-line scratches or blemishes. A paint program cannot support vector graphics, instead it will only work with a bitmap image

compare with
VECTOR

Paintbrush/Paint

application supplied with Microsoft Windows 3.1x and Windows 95 that lets you create or edit bitmap images

see also
BITMAP

palette

range of colours that can be used in a paint program or printed on a colour printer

palmtop computer

tiny computer that is normally about the same size as a paperback book and contains a compact keyboard, screen and storage. For example, the Psion Organiser is a palmtop computer with a keyboard and screen that will run database, wordprocessor and spreadsheet applications.

see also
WINDOWS CE

paragraph

section of text between two carriage returns. In Word, a double click will select a word, a triple click selects the line and four rapid clicks selects the paragraph.

parallel port

connection at the back of your PC that lets you connect your computer to a printer. A parallel port sends data to the printer over eight parallel wires wrapped into one cable and are therefore eight times faster than a serial connection in which the data is sent sequentially.

parameter

information that defines an option or function. For example, if you type in 'DIR /P' at the MS-DOS prompt, the '/P' parameter instructs the DIR command to list all files, pausing between each full screen.

parent folder

folder that contains other folders.

parity

method of checking for errors in a data transmission; there are two systems - odd and even parity. The number of bits equal to '1' in a section of data are counted by the sender and an extra bit is set according to this number. In an error detection system that uses even parity, the extra bit is set to create an even number of bits
see also
EVEN PARITY, ODD PARITY

parity bit

extra bit that is set according to the number of '1' bits in a section of data

partition

way of dividing a hard disk into separate chunks that can then be addressed by separate disk drive letters. For example, if you buy a large 800Mb hard disk, you might find it convenient to split it into four 200Mb partitions that are then called C:, D:, E:, and F:.

password

secret word or phrase that is associated with your user name and confirms your identity. If you subscribe to an online service, such as CompuServe, you will have a public user name and number and a secret password that only you know.

paste

to insert a section of text or other information that was previously copied or cut onto the Clipboard. For example, to move a section of text in a document: select the text, choose Edit/Cut, move to its new location and choose Edit/Paste.

Paste Special

to insert a special object within a document; Windows allows you to insert sound, images, or data from other applications (such as a spreadsheet) into a document. To insert a special object, select Edit/Paste Special
see also
OLE

patch

small program that will fix an error within a larger program.

path

series of directories or folders that locate a particular file. For example, if a file is in a sub-folder LETTERS within a parent folder SIMON, on drive D:, its full path is D:\SIMON\LETTERS

PC
PERSONAL COMPUTER

normally refers to an IBM-compatible computer that is based on an Intel processor. Originally, the term referred to an IBM PC that used an 8088 processor with 512Kb or 640Kb of memory - now this means any computer that runs MS-DOS or Windows; in some cases, PC also means any small computer including the Apple Macintosh.

PC-compatible

software or hardware that will work on a standard IBM-compatible computer that uses an Intel processor and has standard ports and expansion slots.

PCI

PERIPHERAL COMPONENT INTERCONNECT

high-speed local bus designed by Intel that runs at 33MHz and is most often used in Pentium-based personal computers for network or graphics adapters. This high-speed connection on the motherboard of your PC can be used by components that need to exchange large chunks of information at high speed. For example, a graphics adapter could communicate with the processor and main memory at high speed over a PCI connection.

compare with
VESA

PCL

PRINTER CONTROL LANGUAGE

type of page description language that was created by Hewlett Packard and is used in almost all its printers and those of many of its competitors.

PCM

PULSE-CODE MODULATION

way of storing sounds in an accurate, compact format that's used by high-end sound cards.

PCMCIA

PERSONAL COMPUTER MEMORY CARD INTERNATIONAL ASSOCIATION

specification that defines a way of creating tiny peripherals that can be used on laptops and notebook computers. A PCMCIA card is like a fat credit card and has a connector at one end; it fits into a slot in a notebook or laptop and can provide a tiny hard disk drive, modem, network adapter and many other functions and is ideal for those who want to expand the functions of a notebook

PCX file

method of storing a bitmap graphic image file on disk. The standard is widely used and is a convenient way of exchanging graphic files between different paint programs.

PD

see
PUBLIC DOMAIN

PDA

PERSONAL DIGITAL ASSISTANT

palmtop computer that aims to provide all your day-to-day computing and communication requirements. This normally includes a wordprocessor, diary, database, email links, modem and fax within a device the size of a paperback book. Well known examples are the Apple Newton and the Psion Organiser

PDF

PORTABLE DOCUMENT FORMAT
file format used by Adobe Acrobat
see
ADOBE ACROBAT

PDL

see
PAGE DESCRIPTION LANGUAGE

peer

single computer linked to a peer-to-peer network; each peer computer can share
files or resources on other peer computers and can make its own resources available
to the other computers on the network

peer-to-peer network

way of connecting several computers together within an office or building so that
you can exchange files or messages with another user on another computer that is
connected to the network; this system does not use a central, dedicated server;
instead each computer is connected to the next in line and each runs network
software that allows it to share the resources of any other computer on the network.
For example, if you have four computers running Windows 95 you can connect
them together to form a simple peer-to-peer network to allow the four users to share
files, share a printer and exchange electronic mail messages - all using the
networking functions built into Windows

pen computer

small, handheld computer that does not normally have a keyboard, instead a user
operates it using a pen to draw or point on the sensitive display; many PDAs, such
as the Apple Newton, now use a pen to allow a user to write text directly on to the
screen; Microsoft has also developed a version of Windows (called Windows CE)
that can be used in these handheld computers and operates with a pen rather than a
mouse

Pentium™

processor developed by Intel and used in high-performance PCs. It replaced the
80486 and is compatible with all the older 80x86 processor range, and provides
high-speed processing power; however this processor has been replaced by newer
designs including the Pentium Pro.

Pentium Pro™

currently the most powerful processor developed by Intel; this processor replaced
the Pentium for high-performance PCs

peripheral

any add-on item that connects to your computer, such as a printer or modem.

peripheral component interconnect

see
PCI

Perl

programming language normally used to create CGI programs that can process
forms or carry out functions on a Web server; for example, if you want to add a

form or search function to your web server, you could write a program using the Perl language - this program is run by the web server

permanent swap file
file stored on your hard disk, made up of contiguous disk sectors, which is used to store temporary data and pages from the virtual memory system that's used by Windows. If you start several programs running, for example Paint, WordPad and a big application such as Microsoft Excel, then Windows will use virtual memory (which is actually the permanent swap file stored on the disk) to store the programs that it cannot fit into the real RAM chips installed in your PC. Windows 3.x supports either permanent or temporary swap files, but a permanent file is faster - you can change the size and the file type from a temporary to a permanent swap file using the Control Panel icon in Windows, and selecting the Enhanced/Virtual Memory option. A general rule is that a permanent swap file is faster than a temporary swap file, but it takes up a section of disk space. A temporary swap file is deleted after it's been used, which is important if you are running short of disk space. Windows 95 prefers to keep control of the swap file internally and does not allow a user to vary the size of the permanent swap file

personal computer
see
PC

Personal Computer Memory Card International Association
see
PCMCIA

personal digital assistant
see
PDA

personal information manager (PIM)
software that helps a user to organise their diary, appointments, address book and projects; Windows 95 includes the Schedule+ PIM utility that provides diary and address book features and Microsoft Office 97 includes the more sophisticated Outlook program that combines these features with electronic mail

personalizing
term used by Microsoft that means you can change the settings of Windows from their default. For example, you can change the background wallpaper to display a different image behind your windows or you could change the colours of the title bars, the font used by Windows and so on. To make these changes, use the Control Panel icon in the Main program group of Windows 3.1x or the Start/Settings menu item in Windows 95.

perspective
appearance of depth in an image in which objects that are further away from the viewer appear smaller - there is a new range of cheap 3-D software programs that let you add perspective to your images or to text.

PgDn
see
PAGE DOWN KEY

PGP
PRETTY GOOD PRIVACY

encryption system developed to allow anyone to protect the contents of their email messages from unauthorised readers; this system is often used when sending credit card or payment details over the internet

PgUp
see
PAGE UP KEY

phase alternation line (PAL)
standard for television transmission and reception using a 625-line picture transmitted at 25 frames per second; PAL provides a clearer image than NTSC and is used in most of Europe, except for France which uses SECAM. The USA and Japan use NTSC

Phone Dialer
utility supplied with Windows 95 that allows you to dial telephone numbers from the comfort of your computer. In order to use this utility, you need to have a modem installed and connected to the telephone network, plus a normal telephone handset to use once you have dialled the number.

phoneme
one small sound, several of which may make up a spoken word; used to analyse voice input to recognise words or to produce speech by playing back a sequence of phonemes

phono connector *or* RCA connector
plug and socket standard used to connect audio and video devices; the male plug has a 1/8-inch metal central core that sticks out from within the centre of an insulated core. If you have fitted a sound card to your PC you'll see two phono connectors on the back plate. These let you connect your sound card directly to your HiFi or tape recorder.

phosphor
substance that produces light when excited by some form of energy, usually an electron beam. Phosphor is used for coating the inside of a monitor (the cathode ray tube); a thin layer of phosphor is arranged in a pattern of tiny dots on the inside of the screen and produces an image when scanned by the picture beam. In a colour screen there are three tiny coloured phosphor dots (coloured red, green and blue) arranged in a group; the different colours you see displayed are a mix of the light from the three dots.

phosphor dots
individual dots of red, green and blue phosphor on the inside of a colour screen

PhotoCD™
standard developed to store 35mm photographic slides or negatives in digital format on a CD-ROM. The PhotoCD is normally created at the same time as the photographic film is developed - by digitizing each frame at a resolution of 2048x3072 pixels with 24bit colour (together with a lower-resolution preview image file); one PhotoCD can hold 100 photographs. To read a PhotoCD disc, the CD-ROM drive must conform to the CD-ROM XA standard. If all the images are recorded onto the PhotoCD at the same time, then the disc can be read by a single-

session drive; if further images are recorded onto the PhotoCD at a later date, then the disc can only be read by a multi-session CD-ROM drive (developed by Kodak and Philips). If you want to display photographs on your PC, the simplest and cheapest way is to use the PhotoCD system. Take photographs with a normal colour film and ask for a PhotoCD disc when you take the film in to the chemist (this service is normally only from the bigger chemists or photographic shops). You will receive the pictures as normal together with a CD-ROM which has graphic files of the pictures and can be accessed from your CD-ROM drive.

photorealistic
computer image that has almost the same quality and clarity as a photograph; for example, images stored on a PhotoCD are photorealistic since they are scanned at a resolution of 2048x3072 pixels in 24-bit colour

phototypesetter
device that can produce very high-resolution text on photo-sensitive paper or film; the phototypesetter, rather like a large laser printer, normally uses the PostScript page description language and can generate type at 2,540 dpi; if the device is capable of outputting text and half-tone images, it is normally called an image setter. If you want to produce a professional-looking newsletter or brochure, you would send a disk of the files to a bureau that has a phototypesetter machine; the bureau will produce a printed version that you can then give to a printer.

pica
i) measurment equal to 12points (0.166 inch).
ii) width of characters in a typeface, usually 12 characters to the inch

pico- (p)
prefix meaning one trillionth

picture element
see
PIXEL

PIF
see
PROGRAM INFORMATION FILE

PIM
see
PERSONAL INFORMATION MANAGER

pin
metal wire or metal conducting leg on a chip or other electronic device

pincushion distorsion
fault with a monitor that causes the distorsion of an image displayed in which the edges curve in towards the centre. Some monitors have controls to adjust the display to get rid of pincushion distorsion - otherwise if a straight line or edge of a window displayed close to the edge of the monitor appears curved you should return the monitor to the manufacturers.

PING
software utility that will test all the nodes on a network or internet to ensure that

they are working correctly. If you use the internet, you might see a message saying 'PING tests' - these mean that the ISP has tested its connections to other computers.

pipe

to create a link between two programs running on a computer so that the output of one program is sent as input to the other; in MS-DOS you can create a pipe between two DOS utilities using the '|' symbol

pipeline burst cache

secondary synchronous cache that uses very high speed memory chips (with access speeds of around 9ns); the main feature of this type of cache is that it transfers large amounts of data in bursts during a CPU clock cycle

pipelining

i) method of executing several instructions in parallel to increase performance. Some new high-performance computers use pipelining or pipeline memory to try and boost performance by executing several instructions at once.

ii) to carry out more than one task at a time: for example, to compress and store an image on disk as it is being scanned .

pirate

to illegally copy commercial software applications

pitch

i) number of characters which will fit into one inch of line, when the characters are typed in single spacing (used on line-printers, the normal pitches available being 10, 12 and 17 characters per inch).

ii) frequency of a sound

pixel or picture element

smallest single unit or point on a display or on a printer whose colour or brightness can be controlled. A monitor normally has a resolution of 72 pixels per inch, whereas a laser printer has a resolution of 300-600 pixels (also called dots) per inch.

plane

(in a graphics image) one layer of an image that can be manipulated independently within a graphics program. Many drawing programs let you create different planes or layers within your drawing and edit the layers independently.

plasma display or gas plasma display

display screen using the electroluminescing properties of certain gases to display text; this is a thin display usually used in small portable computers
compare with
LCD, TFT

platform

type of hardware or combination of hardware and system software that makes up a particular range of computers. For example, the PC-compatible platform usually means a computer that has an Intel-compatible 80x86 or Pentium processor running DOS, Windows 95 or another popular operating system. When you buy a new piece of software, the side of the box normally lists the type of platform that the software requires to run. This might be either the type of hardware, the amount of RAM or the operating system that is required.

platform independence
software that can work with different types of incompatible hardware. For example, some software, such as Adobe's Acrobat graphics format, can be displayed on a Macintosh and a PC.

platter
one disc in a hard disk drive; a hard disk drive normally has between two and eight separate discs (platters) mounted on a central metal rod (the spindle)

playback
to run a multimedia title or view a video clip or listen to a recorded sound

playback head
electronic device that reads signals recorded on a storage medium and usually converts them to an electrical signal

playback rate scale factor
i) (in waveform audio) sound played back at a different rate, directed by another application, to create a special effect - created by skipping samples rather than changing the sample rate.

ii) (video displayed on a computer) point at which video playback is no longer smooth and appears jerky due to missed frames; this is determined by the size of the playback window and the power of the processor. The first time you view a video clip on your computer, the software (normally Video for Windows) will analyse the speed of your computer and will work out the playback rate that it should use to display video action that appears smooth.

plotter
printing device that creates an image on paper using a pen to draw onto the paper

Plug and Play™ (PNP)
development in PCs that is part of the Windows 95 system: it is a combination of hardware and software. The way it works is complex, but the result is simple: when you plug a new adapter card (a new disk controller, network adapter or graphics adapter) into your PC you don't have to configure it or set any switches - when you next switch on the PC, Windows it will automatically configure and set up the new adapter for you. This process works with Windows 95 and adapters that conform to the Plug and Play standard (also sometimes called PNP).

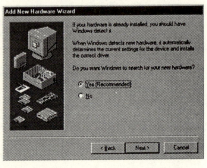

plug-compatible
equipment that can work with several different types of computer, so long as they have the correct type of connector. For example, a SCSI hard disk drive will work with any computer that has a SCSI controller card - you could even switch a drive from a Macintosh to a PC.

plug-in
program that works with a Web browser to increase the functionality of the

browser; for example, if you want to view Adobe Acrobat pages from your Web browser you will need to get the Adobe plug-in that will then be used to view the pages

see also
BROWSER

PNP

see
PLUG AND PLAY

point

i) to move an on-screen cursor using a mouse or arrow keys; see also pointer
ii) (typography) a unit of measurement equal to 1/72-inch - normally used to measure the height of a character

point of presence

see
POP

pointer

graphical symbol - normally a small arrow - used to indicate the position of a cursor on a display. If you are using Windows, the pointer changes shape according to what you are doing. For example, it is normally an arrow, but would change to an I-beam pointer when you are typing or editing.

pointing device

input device that controls the position of a cursor on screen. The most common example is a mouse, which controls the position of a pointer as you move the mouse; other examples are touchpads - common on laptop computers - that move the pointer as you move your finger over a sensitive pad.

point to point protocol

see
PPP

policy

see
ACCEPTABLE USER POLICY

polygon

graphics shape with three or more sides

POP
POINT OF PRESENCE

telephone access number for a service provider that you can use to connect to the internet via your modem. Most of the big service providers have dozens of POPs scattered across the country so that you can connect to the internet with a local-rate telephone call. If you are trying to decide on a service provider, make sure that it has a POP near you or you will have to pay higher telephone charges if you are in Cornwall and its only POP is in Dundee. If you travel, check if the service provider has any POPs overseas or you will have to telephone a UK or home long distance telephone number to get onto the internet.

see also
ISP

POP 3

system used to transfer electronic mail messages between a user's computer and a server (at an ISP).

see also
SMTP

pop-up menu

menu that can be displayed on the screen at any time by pressing the appropriate key, usually displayed over material already on the screen; once the user has made a choice from the menu, it disappears and the original screen display is restored. This rather dry definition is best illustrated with an example, for example, if you use Windows you are probably using pull-down menus (select the Start button or File menu and you are using a pull-down menu) which appears below a menu option. Pop-up menus are used in DOS programs and in a few Windows applications.

pop-up window

window that can be displayed on the screen at any time on top of anything that is already on the screen; when the window is removed, the original screen display is restored. These are most often used to display warning messages or to confirm a choice. For example, if (under Windows) you try and save a file with a name that is the same as an existing file, you'll see a pop-up window that asks if you want to overwrite the existing file or change the name - these pop-up windows are often called dialog boxes.

populate

to insert electronic chips into empty sockets on a motherboard, normally to upgrade your computer by adding more memory

port

i) to transfer an application between platforms.

ii) communications channel that allows a computer to exchange data with a peripheral. On the the back of your computer you'll see a range of connectors - these are all ports between your computer and the outside world.

See also
PRINTER PORT, SERIAL PORT.

iii) (on the internet) number assigned to each program that runs on a network server; normally you do not need to know this number, but sometimes you might need to access a program directly (such as when using Telnet) and in this case you would access the port

portable

i) compact self-contained computer that can be carried around and used either with a battery pack or mains power supply.

see also
LAPTOP

ii) (any hardware or software or data files) that can used on a range of different computers. For example, Adobe's Acrobat graphics file format can be viewed on almost any type of computer.

portable document format

see
PDF

portrait

orientation of a page or piece of paper where the longest edge is vertical. If you want to change the way in which a page is printed, you should use the File/Print Setup/Setup option in you application which allows you to change the orientation and size of the paper used.

compare with
LANDSCAPE

post office

central store for the messages for users on a local area network; the post office will also ensure that messages are delivered locally and might have a gateway to route any mail to other post offices or mail systems

PostScript

language used to describe how a printed page will look - including the size, position and style of text and graphics. PostScript was developed by Adobe Systems and offers flexible font sizing and positioning; it is most often produced by DTP systems and used in high-quality laser printers and phototypesetters; Display PostScript is an extension of PostScript that allows PostScript commands to be displayed on a screen so that a user can see exactly what will appear on the printer. An encapsulated PostScript file contains PostScript commands that describe an image or page, the commands are stored in a file and this can be placed on a page; an encapsulated PostScript file often contains a preview image in TIFF format

power management

software built into laptop computers and some newer desktop PCs and monitors that will automatically turn-off components that are not being used to save energy. Power management is designed to cut the electrical power supply to a device or peripheral when it's not being used. For example, if the computer has not been used for 10 minutes, the power management software might cut power to the disk drive (which normally spins constantly) or to the monitor. As soon as you hit a key or move the mouse, the power is re-supplied to the device and your computer 'wakes up' again. In a laptop, it's a good way of conserving the battery power and can often double the effective life of a battery.

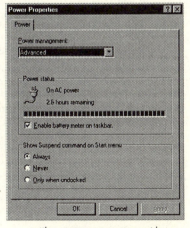

setting up power management in
Windows 95

see also
ENERGY STAR

power down

to turn off the electricity supply to a computer or other electronic device
see also
SHUTDOWN

PowerPC™

high-performance RISC-based processor developed by Motorola and used in the PowerPC range of Apple Macintosh computers and in some graphics workstations and top-of-the-range PCs and Apple Macintosh computers.

power supply
electrical device in a computer that converts the mains electrical supply to a steady DC voltage of (normally) 5volts and 12volts that is then used to provide electricity to the disk drives and electronic components in the computer

power up
to turn on the electricity supply to a computer or other electronic device

power user
user who needs the latest, fastest model of computer because he runs complex or demanding applications

ppm
see
PAGES PER MINUTE

PPP
POINT TO POINT PROTOCOL
set of commands that allow a computer to use the TCP/IP protocol over a telephone connection. Normally, the TCP/IP will only work over a network, but the PPP system fools it into working over a telephone line. You might wonder what this has to do with you! The TCP/IP protocol is the way in which computers talk to other computers over the internet, so you need to use the PPP system if you want to connect to the internet using a modem.

preemptive multitasking
feature of some operating systems (notably IBM OS/2 and Microsoft Windows 95) that allows them to run several programs at the same time in an efficient manner. The trick is that with preemptive multitasking, the operating system is always in control: it executes a program for a period of time, then passes control to the next program so preventing any one program using all the processor time.

prescan
feature of many flat-bed scanners that carry out a quick, low-resolution scan to allow you to re-position the original or mark the area that is to be scanned at a higher resolution

presentation graphics
graphics that have been created to display business information or data. Presentation graphics are normally created in slides that can then be displayed on an overhead projector or direct on a PC monitor. If you are giving a lecture or trying to sell a product or giving a presentation on the latest company sales figures, each slide in the presentation graphics would illustrate a point or would show graphs or images to back up your speech. You can create your own presentation graphics using either a sophisticated wordprocessor or a paint program, but special presentation graphics software makes it easier to create slides and normally includes hundreds of logos and icons to make the slides more exciting.

Presentation Manager
graphical user interface supplied with the OS/2 operating system, that is similar to

Windows, but includes slightly different utilities

presentation software
software application that allows a user to create a business presentation with graphs, data, text and images

pretty good privacy
see
PGP

preview
to display text or graphics on a screen as it will appear when it is printed out. Wordprocessors, such as Microsoft Word, have a standard view which allows you to type and edit rapidly. However, if you want to see the effect of margins, tables or columns, you would switch to preview mode which shows exactly how the page will look when printed.

primitive
(in graphics) simple shape (such as circle, square, line, curve) used to create more complex shapes in a graphics program

print
to produce characters on paper using ink or toner

print control code
special character sent to a printer that directs it to perform an action or function (such as change font), rather than print a character

print job
file in a print queue that contains all the characters and printer control codes needed to print one document or page

print life
number of characters a component can print before needing to be replaced. For example, a laser printer toner cartridge normally has a print life of around 5,000 pages.

Print Manager
software utility that is part of Microsoft Windows and is used to manage print queues

print modifiers
special codes included in a document that cause a printer to change mode, i.e. from bold to italic

print preview
function of a software product that lets the user see how a page will appear when printed
see
PREVIEW

print queue
list of the files waiting to be printed. If you are using Windows, the printing is normally controlled by the Print Manager - a program that will accept any

document that an application wants to print and temporarily stores it on disk until the printer has finished the previous document.

Print Screen key

special key in the top right-hand side of the keyboard that under DOS will send the characters that are displayed on the screen to the printer. Under Windows, its function has changed and it now copies the screen image to the Clipboard. For example, if you want to produce a manual for other users or want to print part of the Windows screen, press the Print Screen key. Now start the Paint program (from the Accessories group) and choose the Edit/Paste menu option. A copy of the image that was displayed on screen is copied into the Paint file and can be printed or edited. If you want to copy an image of the active window (the window that has a dark blue title bar and is currently being used) rather than the whole screen, press the Alt and PrintScreen keys at the same time. If you want to see what you have captured, use the Clipbook Viewer utility that is in the Accessories group.

print server

computer in a network that is connected to a printer and stores the print queue with temporary files before they are printed.

see also
SERVER

print spooling

to automatically print a number of different documents in a queue at the normal speed of the printer, while the computer is doing some other task

printer

device that produces text or an image on paper using ink or toner under the control of a computer. There are many different kinds of printer: a daisy-wheel printer is an impact printer that strikes an inked ribbon with a metal impression of a character arranged on interchangeable daisy-wheels. A dot-matrix printer forms characters from a series of tiny dots printed close together; an ink-jet printer produces characters by sending a stream of tiny drops of electrically charged ink onto the paper (the movement of the ink drops is controlled by an electric field); a laser printer is a high-resolution printer that uses a laser source to print high quality dot-matrix characters normally at a resolution of 300 or 600dpi; a line-printer prints text one character at a time, moving horizontally across each line; a page printer composes one page of text, then prints it rapidly (such as a laser printer). A printer is normally connected to the parallel port at the back of your computer, but some printers will connect to the serial port (which is much slower at transferring data to the printer). When you connect a new printer to your PC you must tell the software - Windows - the type of printer you are using. Each printer is controlled by slightly different control codes and so each printer needs a printer driver - a special file that tells Windows how to control this particular printer. Before using a new printer you must install a new printer driver using the Printers icon in the Control Panel. If you are using Windows 95, it will automatically detect that a new printer has been connected and will try and work out the type of printer.

printer buffer

temporary store for character data waiting to be printed; a printer buffer is used to release an application to continue working rather than wait for a slow printer that is printing the work

printer control language
see
PCL

printer driver
special file that tells Windows how to control a particular printer. For example, a PostScript printer such as a Hewlett Packard LaserJet 4M needs to receive data as PostScript instructions whereas an ink-jet printer needs to receive data as instructions that tell it how to print one line at a time. These differences are translated by the printer driver which sits between Windows and the printer. Windows comes with hundreds of printer drivers supplied - these cover most existing printers - however if a new printer is produced make sure that it is supplied with a Windows printer driver or you will not be able to print! The exception is if the printer is emulating another type of printer. For example, all PostScript printers can use the same basic PostScript printer driver.

printer emulation
printer that is able to interpret the standard set of commands used to control another brand of printer .

printhead
i) row of needles in a dot-matrix printer that produce characters as a pattern of dots.
ii) metal form of a character that is pressed onto an inked ribbon to print the character on paper.
iii) in an ink-jet printer, a plastic cartridge of ink together with a row of tiny holes that is used to squirt the drops of ink onto the paper.

printout
final printed page

PRN
PRINTER
acronym used in MS-DOS to represent the standard printer port. For example, if you are at the DOS prompt (C:\>) and want to print a text file, such as the CONFIG.SYS file, you could enter the command 'TYPE CONFIG.SYS < PRN' which will send the contents of the CONFIG.SYS file to the printer. This won't work if you have a PostScript printer, which expects data in the form of PostScript commands.

processing
series of actions that a computer carries out to arrive at a result

processor
electronic device that provides the functions that control your computer. A processor is an electronic device that contains millions of tiny electronic components that have been designed to carry out basic arithmetic and control functions. A CPU can add or subtract two numbers, move numbers from one memory location to another or control an external device. Each of the actions of a CPU is controlled by an instruction - these are the machine code instructions that are used to create software programs. The specification of a CPU is defined in several ways: its speed (for example, current high-speed PCs use a processor that runs with a clock speed of 200MHz) roughly defines the number of instructions that it can process each second - 200 million in this case. The power of a CPU is also defined in its data handling capabilities: a 32-bit CPU can add, subtract or

manipulate numbers that are 32-bits wide. A 16-bit processor can only handle 16-bit numbers, so would take twice as long to deal with a big number. Lastly, there are two main families of CPU. The Intel-developed range of CPUs is the 80386, 80486 and Pentium. These are used in PCs and are backwards compatible. Other manufacturers, such as AMD, are licensed to manufacture these CPUs and they work in exactly the same way. The second main family is the 68000 and PowerPC range from Motorola. These are used in Apple computers and are not directly compatible with the Intel range.

see also
CPU, NUMERIC COPROCESSOR

profile
feature of Windows 95 that stores the settings for different users on one PC. This is normally used in companies, but could solve a lot of arguments at home! Each user has his or her own profile that describes how Windows looks and performs for each user. For example, Simon might want shortcuts to an internet browser on the Desktop, wheras Sue might prefer to keep clear of the internet and have CD-ROM titles installed as shortcuts. When you switch on the PC, Windows asks for your user name and configures itself according to the settings in the Profile. If you want to try out this feature, make sure that you read the user manuals carefully beforehand for a full explanation.

PROFS
electronic mail standard, developed by IBM, built into OfficeVision, allowing users to send messages over a network

program
i) complete set of instructions which direct a computer to carry out a particular task. For example, a wordprocessing software package is actually tens of thousands of separate instructions that respond to your various actions (such as printing, spell-check or formatting text). These instructions are written by a programmer who creates the program file that contains all the instructions. A program file normally has an extension of .EXE (or .COM for some programs).
ii) (in MIDI) data that defines a sound in a synthesizer; sometimes called a patch

program group
(in Windows 3.1x) window that contains icons relating to a particular subject or program - it's a convenient way of organising your files. For example, the Accessories icon opens the Accessories program group window that contains icons for the various utilities that are included with Windows, such as Paint, Write and so on. In Windows 95, the program groups no longer exist. Instead, there are program folders and program menu trees. Each program folder becomes a sub-menu of the Start/Programs menu.

program icon
icon that represents a program file; to start the program, move the pointer over the icon and double-click on the program icon.

program information file (PIF)
(in Microsoft Windows) file that contains the environment settings for a particular program; the environment settings include the amount of memory the program requires, the way in which in handles graphics and printers and disk space. Windows normally sets these options to standard values.

program instruction

single word or expression that represents one operation. For example, the program instruction ADD A,B adds the values of A and B. It gets a little more confusing when you consider the types of programming language: high level programming languages such as Visual Basic are easier to use, but each program instruction is actually made up of several low-level intructions.

see also
PROGRAMMING LANGUAGE

Program Manager

(In Windows 3.x) main part of Windows that the user sees; when you start Windows you'll see a background and a main window with icons and smaller windows contained within it. This main window is the Program Manager and it allows you to format a disk, run an application or carry out similar basic housekeeping commands. In Windows 95, Microsoft scrapped Program Manager. Instead, the screen is now taken up by the Desktop. This contains icons for the different disk drives, options to format or view disks and so on.

programmable key

key on a keyboard that can be assigned a particular function

programming language

description of a series of instructions and commands that can be used by a programmer to create a software application; to write a program with a programming language, a programmer uses software that allows him to enter a series of instructions to define a particular task, which will then be translated to a form that is understood by the computer. Programming languages are grouped into different levels: the high-level languages such as BASIC and PASCAL are easy to understand and use, but offer slow execution time since each instruction is made up of a number of machine code instructions; low-level languages (such as assembler) are more complex to read and program in, but offer faster execution time

Programs menu

sub-menu that's accessed from the Start button in Windows 95. The Programs menu lists all the programs you have installed on your computer and lets you start any program by selecting the menu item. The alternative and more fiddly way to start a program is to open the MyComputer icon on the Desktop, double-click on the C-drive icon, select the correct folder for the program and then, finally, double-click on the program file.

prompt

message or character displayed to remind the user that an input is expected; for example, DOS uses the 'C:\>' command prompt to indicate that a command is expected - in the case of DOS, the command prompt also displays the name of the current disk and the name of the current subdirectory. For example, if you change directory to \letters, the prompt will now look like 'C:\letters\>'.

properties

(In Windows 95) attributes of a file or object. To view or edit all the properties of a file, select the file (with a single click to highlight the name) and click once on the right-hand mouse button. This displays a small menu of options - select the Properties menu option and you will see the various properties for the object. If the object is a file, you can view or edit the attributes to make the file read-only or hidden. You can also change the name or location of an object.

proportional spacing
way of displaying or printing text so that each letter takes a space proportional to the character width (so that 'i' takes up less space than 'm'). This makes the text look neater when displayed, but can cause problems if you want to line up columns; in this case you should either tabulate the text or use a monospaced font such as Courier.
compare
MONOSPACED

protected mode
operating mode of an Intel processor (the 80286 or higher) that supports multitasking, virtual memory, and data security
compare with
REAL MODE

protocol
set of pre-defined codes and signals that allow two different pieces of hardware to communicate. For example, a simple protocol ensures that data is correctly transferred from a computer to a printer along the printer cable; other protocols ensure that a computer can communicate via the internet or over a network. A protocol is equivalent to a spoken language. If you cannot get two computers to exchange information, it's likely that they are using different communications protocols

proxy server
computer that stores copies of files and data normally held on a slow server and so allows users to access files and data quickly

PrtSc
PRINT SCREEN
(on an IBM PC keyboard) key that sends the contents of the current screen to the printer or copies a Windows screen to the Clipboard

PS/2
range of personal computers developed by IBM
see also
MICROCHANNEL ARCHITECTURE

pseudo-static
dynamic RAM memory chips that contain circuitry to refresh the contents and so have the same appearance as a static RAM component

public domain (PD)
documents or images or sound or text or programs that have no copying fee or restrictions and can be used or copied by anyone. Public domain is rare, since it means that there is no copyright. More usual is freeware, in which the author retains copyright, but allows distribution and use for free.
compare with
SHAREWARE

public key encryption
method of encrypting data that uses one key to encrypt the data and another different key to decrypt the data; the key used to encrypt is made public to any one that wants

to send you an encrypted message, but you keep the decryption key secret
see also
PGP

publish

i) to produce and sell software.

ii) to design edit, print and sell books or magazines; computers and multimedia have greatly influenced how works are published: desktop publishing (DTP) is the design, layout and printing of documents using special software, a small computer and a printer, while electronic publishing uses computers to write and display information (such as viewdata or CD-ROM titles).

iii) to share a local resource with other users on a network (such as a file or folder).

iv) to place web pages on a web server so that users can view the pages on the internet

pull-down menu

set of options that are displayed below the relevant entry on a menu-bar. If you click on the Start button in Windows 95 or on the File menu in Windows 3.x you'll see an example of a pull-down menu.

pulse-code modulation

see
PCM, ADPCM

pulse-dialling

method of dialling a telephone number that uses a number of pulses to dial a digit. For example, if you dial three, pulse dialling will send three pulses. This is an old-fashioned and slow method of dialling. Just about every telephone exchange can now use tone-dialling which is much faster: each digit has a different tone.

purge

to empty the contents of the Recycle Bin in Windows 95; click once on the Bin icon, then click on the right-hand mouse button and choose the Empty option.

push-button

square shape displayed on a screen that will carry out a particular action if selected; a push-button is normally made up of two images: one appears as if the button is protruding from the screen, the second, displayed when the button is selected, that is shaded differently to appear to sink into the screen

Qq

quad-speed drive
CD-ROM drive that spins the disc at four times the speed of a single-speed drive, providing higher data throughput of 600Kbps and shorter seek times. Quad-speed drives are now standard on most new PCs and, for high-performance PCs, have been superseded by six-speed drives.

quantize
i) to convert an analog signal into a numerical representation.

ii) to process a MIDI file and align all the notes to a regular beat, so removing any timing errors

query
question entered into a search engine to retrieve selected documents from a database

query window
i) window that appears when an error has occured, asking the user what action he would like to take.

ii) window that is displayed with fields a user can fill in to search a database

question mark (?)
question mark is normally used in searches and is called a wildcard and means 'any character'. So, 'Print?' will match with 'Print' and 'Prints' but not with 'Printed'. To search for all three of these terms, you could use 'Print??'. Alternatively, you could use the asterisk '*' which means 'any number of any characters'. The question mark is also used in DOS and is useful when finding files that match a certain criteria. It's normally used with the DIR command; for example 'DIR print?.*' will display all the files that start 'print' and have any type of file extension. This would match 'Print.DOC', 'Print.TXT', and 'Prints.TXT'.

queue
collection of documents waiting to be printed

quoting
feature of many electronic mail applications that allows you to reply to a message and include the text of the original message; to distinguish the original text, each line normally starts with a '>' symbol

QWERTY keyboard
English language keyboard layout for a typewriter or computer, in which the top line of letters are QWERTY. The French use a different layout with the keys on the top line reading AZERTY.

Rr

radio button

circle displayed beside an option that, when selected, has a dark centre; radio buttons are a method of selecting one of a number of options, only one radio button in a group can be selected at any time (select another in the group and the first is deselected)

ragged

text that is not straight or aligned and has an uneven edge

ragged left

printed or displayed text that lines up flush on the right-hand margin but has an uneven left-hand margin

ragged right

printed or displayed text that lines up flush on the left-hand margin but has an uneven right-hand margin

RAID

REDUNDANT ARRAY OF INEXPENSIVE DISKS

storage device that consists of a set of hard disk drives and is used in high-performance PCs or in network servers. The idea is that instead of using one big disk drive, it's more reliable to use eight cheap smaller drives and add one spare in case of a fault. The whole lot are packaged in a case. RAIDs are all the rage at the moment, so you will see a lot of advertisements with this term. It's not particularly useful for home PCs.

RAM

RANDOM ACCESS MEMORY

memory that allows access to any location in any order, without having to access the rest first (the memory chips in your PC are RAM, since any location can be accessed by specifying its address; a magnetic tape is not random access, since you must read through all locations before you reach the one you want to access)

RAM cache

section of high-speed RAM that is used to buffer data transfers between the (faster) processor and a (slower) disk drive

RAMDAC

RANDOM ACCESS DIGITAL TO ANALOG CONVERTER

electronic component on a video graphics adapter that coverts the digital colour signals into electrical signals that are sent to the monitor

RAM disk
see
SILICON DISK

random access memory
see
RAM

range left
move text to align it to the left margin

ray tracing
(in graphics) method of creating life-like computer-generated graphics which correctly show shadows and highlights on an object as if coming from a light source; ray tracing software calculates the direction of each ray of light, its reflection and how it looks on an object

RCA connector
see
PHONO CONNECTOR

RDBMS
RELATIONAL DATABASE MANAGEMENT SYSTEM
database software that lets you define how different fields in different files are related. For example, you might have a database of all your products sorted by their code number. Another file has a list of all your customers. A third file could be used for orders and would retrieve the customer details from the customer file and the product details from the product file.

read only
file or memory device whose stored data cannot be changed. A CD-ROM disc is read-only, in that you cannot save a new version of a file to the CD-ROM as you could to a floppy disk.

read only attribute
attribute bit of a file that, if set, prevents new data being written to the file or its contents edited. If you want to protect a file from being accidentally changed, you could set its attribute to read-only using the ATTRIB command in DOS or using its Properties page in Windows 95.

read only memory (ROM)
type of memory device that has had data written into it at the time of manufacture, and now its contents can only be read. A CD-ROM is normally considered a type of read-only memory since files are usually written to it when it is manufactured (in fact, this is changing since you can now buy personal CD-ROM writers).
see also
EPROM, FLASH ROM

read/write head
see
ACCESS HEAD

readme file
file that contains last-minute information about an application; the file is normally

stored on the disk or CD-ROM together with the application files

RealAudio™

system used to transmit sound over the internet, normally used to transmit live sound, for example from a radio station, over the internet; to use RealAudio, your Web browser needs a special plug-in

see
PLUG-IN

real memory

actual physical memory chips that can be addressed by a CPU

compare with
VIRTUAL MEMORY

real mode

(In an IBM PC) default operating mode and the only mode in which DOS operates; real mode normally means only one program can be written at a time and in which software can use any available memory or I/O device

compare
PROTECTED MODE, WINDOWS

real time

problem in which the processing time to solve the problem is of the same order of magnitude as the problem to be solved. This means that the computer can solve a problem in a certain time and its result can influence the source of the data. A good example is an air traffic control computer - it has to analyse the position of aircraft within a second so that they do not colide. If the computer was not working in real time, it would spend minutes calculating the action, which would be of no use.

real-time animation

computer animation in which objects appear to move at the same speed as they would in real life; real-time animation requires a powerful processor and a graphics adapter that can display a sequence of 20 animated images every second

reboot

to reset your computer, that is equivalent to switching it off then on again. You can reboot your computer using either the Ctrl-Alt-Del key combination or by choosing the Start/Shutdown/Reboot in Windows 95 or by pressing a reset button.

receipt notification

feature of many electronic mail applications that will send you an automatic message to confirm that the recipient has received your message

record

one complete entry in a database that might contain information in many separate fields; for example, in a customer database, information on each customer would be stored in a separate record, which would be made up of different fields for the name and address and order details

record head or write head

transducer that converts an electrical signal into a magnetic field to record data onto a magnetic medium

record locking
system used in database applications to prevent more than one user changing the contents of a record at the same time as another user is looking at the record

recordable CD
see
CD-R

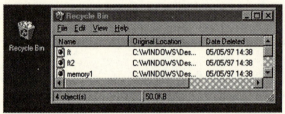

Recycle Bin in Windows 95

Recycle Bin
icon that's displayed on the Windows 95 Desktop that looks like a wastepaper bin. If you want to delete a file or folder, drag it onto the Recycle Bin icon or press the Delete key. The Recycle Bin stores the file or folder for a certain number of days or until you purge the Bin of its contents. The contents of the Bin have not actually been deleted from the disk until you purge it.

red, green, blue (RGB)
i) high-definition monitor system that uses three separate input signals controlling red, green and blue colour picture beams.
ii) the three colour picture beams used in a colour CRT; in a colour TV there are three colour guns producing red, green and blue beams acting on groups of three phosphor dots at each pixel location

reduced instruction set computer (RISC)
type of design of a processor whose instruction set contains a small number of simple fast-executing instructions, that can make program writing more complex, but increases speed of execution of each instruction

redundant array of inexpensive disks
see
RAID

refresh
process to update regularly the images on a CRT screen by scanning each pixel with a picture beam to make sure the image is still visible. The image on the screen is visible because tiny dots of phosphor shine; the glow from the phosphor only lasts a few tenths of a second and so the dots have to be 'hit' by an electron picture beam to get them to glow again. This process is repeated tens (often 60-70) times per second.

refresh rate
number of times every second that the image on a CRT is redrawn. The more times the image is redrawn every second, the less you will see flickering in the image - large screens have to be refreshed at a rate of 60-70 times every second to prevent the screen flickering.

region fill
to fill an area of a screen or a graphics shape with a particular colour - in the Paint

program in Windows there is a paint-can tool that will carry out a region fill of a defined area or shape.

registry

database that forms the basis of Windows 95. The registry contains information about every program that is stored on the disk and the users, networks and preferences. You'll never actually see the registry, but its worth knowing its there in case you see a cryptic error message such as 'Object not found in Registry' which means some program has not been correctly installed. For those intrigued by these things, the registry is the replacement for the old INI files used in Windows 3.x.

rehyphenation

to change the hyphenation of words in a text after it has been put into a new page format or line width

relational database

database that lets you define how different fields in different files are related. For example, you might have a database of all your products sorted by their code number. Another file has a list of all your customers. A third file could be used for orders and would retrieve the customer details from the customer file and the product details from the product file.

relational database management system

see
RDBMS

release

version of a product

remote access

to use your desktop PC from another location with a telephone link. You need two computers, each with a modem, and special remote access software (that is built into Windows 95) and this allows you to dial one computer and access the files and folders on its hard disk as if you were there.

remote client

a user who is accessing mail without being connected to the mail server's local network. The user can be elsewhere in a WAN, or accessing the mail system via a modem link.

REN

RINGER EQUIVALENCE NUMBER
number that defines the load a device places on a telephone network; any device that can be connected to the telephone network has this load number, if you connect equipment to your telephone system you must ensure that the total of all the REN numbers is less than four

renaming

to change the name of a file or folder. In Windows 95, click once on the file or folder that you want to rename and keep the pointer over the icon. After a couple of seconds the description will be surrounded by a box and you can now edit the name. In DOS use the REN command and in Windows 3.1x use the File Manager utility.

rendering
process of colouring and shading a (normally wire-frame or vector object) graphic object so that it looks solid and real

repeat rate
number of times that a character will be entered on screen if you press and hold down one key on the keyboard

repetitive strain injury or repetitive stress injury (RSI)
pain in the arm felt by someone who performs the same movement many times over a certain period, sometimes experienced by people typing a lot or using the mouse for long periods of time - especially if they are not sitting correctly.

replay
to play back or read back data or a signal from a recording

reply
to answer an electronic mail message; this is often featured as a command in email programs and will automatically take information from the original message and, in the new message enter the correct address, copy the subject line from the original message and preface it with 're:' and insert the text of the original text

request for comment
see
RFC

resample
to change the number of pixels used to make up an image; for example, if you scan an image at 400dpi and your printer is only capable of 300 dpi, you could resample the bitmap image to 300dpi, losing some detail but ensuring that what you edit is printed

reset
to return a system to its initial state, to allow a program or process to be started again; hard reset is similar to soft reset but with a few important differences: it is a switch that directly signals the CPU, while soft reset signals the operating system; hard reset clears all memory contents, a soft reset does not affect memory contents; hard reset should always reset the system if a soft reset does not always work

resolution
i) number of pixels that a screen or printer can display per unit area.
ii) difference between two levels that can be differentiated in a digitized signal.
iii) degree of accuracy with which something can be measured or timed

resource
device which is available on a network or on a computer that can be used by an application or system software; this is rather a general term and can mean a disk drive on your PC or a printer connected to another computer on a network.

resource sharing
using something that is on another computer connected to the network. For example, if your company has a network of four PCs and one is connected to a printer, if the user of another PC on the network wants to print, he would be sharing this resource.

restore
to get good files and information from a copy to replace files that have been corrupted on your computer
see also
BACKUP

reverse characters
characters which are displayed in the opposite way to other characters for emphasis (as black on white or white on black, when other characters are the opposite), often used to indicate you have made a selection or that you have control over a particular section of text. For example, in Word, if you click once on a word you place the cursor at that point. Double-click and the word is selected - indicated by reverse characters - click three times and the line is selected; click four times and the paragraph is selected.

reverse video
screen display mode where white and black are reversed.

revert
to return to the previous version of a document, losing any changes that have been made since the document was last saved

RFC
REQUEST FOR COMMENT
document that contains information about a proposed new standard and asks users to look at the document and make any comments; each RFC document is numbered and available to download from many library internet sites

RGB
RED, GREEN, BLUE
i) high-definition monitor system that uses three separate input signals controlling red, green and blue colour picture beams.
ii) the three colour picture beams used in a colour TV; in a colour CRT there are three colour guns producing red, green and blue beams acting on groups of three phosphor dots at each pixel location

RGB monitor
high-definition monitor system that uses three separate input signals controlling red, green and blue colour picture beams; there are both digital and analog RGB monitors, both produce a sharper and clearer image than a composite video display; in a colour CRT there are three colour guns producing red, green and blue beams acting on groups of three phosphor dots at each pixel location

ribbon cable
type of electrical cable that is wide and flat; is is made up of tens of individual insualted wires glued or bonded together to make them more convenient to handle. For example, disk drives are connected to the disk drive controller using a short piece of ribbon cable that is normally 50 wires wide.

rich text format (RTF)
way of storing a document that includes all the commands that describe the page, type, font and formatting; the RTF format allows formatted pages to be exchanged between differerent word processing software

right justify

formatting command in a wordprocessor or desktop publishing software that makes the right hand margin of the text even; the left margin is ragged

right-click menu

small pop-up menu that appears when you click on the right-hand button of a two-button mouse; often used to select formatting or the properties of an object. Windows 95 makes good use of the right-click menu. If you right-click over a blank part of the Desktop you can set the properties of the Desktop or create a new shortcut. If you right-click over a file or folder you can change its properties.

right-hand button

button on the right-hand side of a two or three-button mouse. The left-hand button is used for most selection operations but the right-hand button is now being used more by Windows 95 to select the properties of a file or folder.

ring topology

network architecture in which each node (computer or printer) is connected together in a loop; used in Token Ring network systems

compare with
BUS TOPOLOGY

ringer equivalence number

see
REN

RISC

see
REDUCED INSTRUCTION SET COMPUTER

RJ-11

connector normally used in telephone sockets in the USA; if you travel to and from the USA and want to use your modem you will need a set of adapters to plug into the local telephone sockets

RJ-45

connector used in newer Ethernet local area networks that use twisted pair cabling and do not use coaxial cable

see also
TWISTED PAIR

RLL

RUN LENGTH LIMITED
method of storing data onto the magnetic surface of a hard disk drive that is more effecient than MFM

see also
MFM

ROM cartridge

software, data or font information stored in a ROM chip that is mounted in a cartridge which can easily be plugged into a computer or printer (often used to store extra font data)

ROM
see
READ ONLY MEMORY

root or root directory
topmost directory (on a disk) from which all other directories branch; in DOS and OS/2 and Unix this is represented as a single backslash character. For example, if you want to move to the root directory, you would issue the 'CD \' command in DOS. Confusingly, the root directory actually represents the top of the tree structure. As you move from the root directory to the subdirectories, you are moving into branches.

rot13
simple encoding that is used to scramble offensive messages posted in newsgroups; for example, offensive messages might be labelled 'rot13 reply' and this warns other users that the text has been encoded and that it's likely to be offensive. The encoding system is very simple: if A=1, B=2 and so on, add 13 to each number and display this text. Almost all newsreader applications can decode rot13 messages

router
device that lets you connect your office network server or in-house internet server to the internet via a leased line. You do not need a router for an ISDN or modem connection. A router is a device similar to a bridge but operating at a higher level within the OSI reference model. Routers detect protocols rather than the data they carry and use the destination address to work out the best route for the packet through a complex network. Typically used within WANs, intelligent routers can select whether to use telephone links, LANs, or particular shortcuts through a network.

routine
section of a computer program that carries out a particular function

row
line of printed or displayed characters

RSI
see
REPETITIVE STRAIN INJURY

RTF
see
RICH TEXT FORMAT

RTFM
common abbreviation used in messages to mean 'read the manual'

ruler line
bar displayed on screen that indicates a unit of measurement; often used in design, DTP or word-processor software to help with layout or to set the tab stops.

rules
method of testing incoming messages for certain conditions (such as the name of the sender or the contents) and acting upon them. For example, a rule could define

that any mail from user 'boss' should be moved to the urgent folder.

run around

way in which a DTP or wordprocessing package can fit text around an image on a printed page. For example, if you insert a picture in a document and set its run around to 'nothing' the DTP package will assume the picture is not there and will overprint with text. If you set the run around to one point, the DTP package will leave a gap of one point around the border of the picture and will fit the text around the picture.

Run command

(in Windows) This command lets you type in the name of a program that you want to run or a DOS command your want to execute. To enter a command, select the File/Run menu command from the Program Manager of Windows 3.1x or the Start/Run menu option from Windows 95.

run-time

set of library routines required by an application when it is actually running. The program calls on the library of routines when it is running.

Ss

safe mode
special operating mode of Windows 95 that is automatically selected if Windows 95 detects that there is a problem when starting. The safe mode does not let you do anything within Windows 95 except to try and work out and fix the problem. When you first install Windows 95 you should create a safe mode diskette that contains the initial configuration details for your PC. In case nothing else works, Windows will ask you to insert this diskette and will copy the initial settings over.

sample
measurement of a signal at a point in time, normally used to describe the action of a sound card that is converting a sound or noise into a form that can be stored on disk.

sample rate
number of measurements of a signal that are recorded every second; a PC sound card normally supports one of the following three standard rates: 11,025, 22,050 and 44,100 samples per second (normally written as 11.025KHz, 22.05KHz and 44.1KHz)
see also
ANALOG/DIGITAL CONVERSION, MPC, QUANTIZE

sample size
size of the word used to measure the level of the signal when it is sampled: normally either 8-bit or 16-bit words are used; an 8-bit word means that each sample can be one of 256 separate levels, a 16-bit word can have 65,536 levels and so is more precise for capturing the finer detail in the signal

save
to store a document on a disk under a unique file name. Normally, Windows applications have a Ctrl-S shortcut for this function or you can choose the File/Save menu option.

save as
menu option that allows you to save an open document to disk under a different name or in a different file format. For example, if you have written a message in Word and want to save it in plain text file format so that it can be sent as an electronic mail, you would select the File/SaveAs menu option and save it in a text file format.

scalable font
font that can be displayed or printed in any size, without changing the shape of the font. Each character in a scalable font is described as a set of curves which can then be altered to print characters in just about any size without creating a jagged or

ragged looking character.

see also
OUTLINE FONT

scan

i) (optical) to convert a printed image or photograph into a digital bitmap form.

ii) (in a display) to move a picture beam across a screen, one line at a time, to refresh the image on the CRT.

iii) to convert an optical image (from a video camera) into a digital form by examining each pixel on one line of a frame, then moving down one line

ScanDisk

utility supplied with MS-DOS (which is also part of Windows 95) that will check your hard disk for any problems and will try and correct problems that it finds. You should run ScanDisk once a month to keep your hard disk in shape.

see also
DEFRAG

scanner

device which uses photo-electric cells to convert an image or drawing or photograph or document into graphical data which can be manipulated by a computer; a scanner is connected and controlled by a computer which can then display or process the image data; a flat-bed scanner is a device with a flat sheet of glass on which the image or photograph or document is placed; the scan head moves below the glass and converts the image into data which can be manipulated by a computer; a hand-held scanner is a device that is held in your hand and contains a row of photo-electric cells which, when moved over an image, convert it into data which can be manipulated by a computer

Schedule+™

software program that provides personal information management features, including a diary. The software is included as part of Microsoft Windows 95 but has been superseded by the Outlook software supplied within Microsoft Office 97

scratchpad memory

section of high-speed memory that is used to buffer data being transferred between a fast processor and a slower storage device (such as a disk drive)

screen

i) display device capable of showing a quantity of information, such as a CRT

ii) grid of dots or lines placed between the camera and the artwork, which has the effect of dividing the piicture up into small dots, creating an image which can be used for printing

screen angle

angle at which a screen is set before the photograph is taken (different angles are used for the four process colours so as to avoid a moiré effect); the normal angles are black: 45 degrees; magenta: 75 degrees; yellow: 90 degrees; cyan: 105 degrees

screen attribute

settings that define how each character will be displayed on screen. This includes the background and foreground colours and bold, italic or underline styles.

screen border

margin around text displayed on a screen

screen buffer

temporary storage area of memory chips - usually on a graphics adapter - that store the characters or graphics before they are displayed

screen burn

problem caused if a stationary image is displayed for too long on a monitor, burning the phosphor. This problem was the original reason why screen savers were developed. Now, screens are better made and the phosphor is more resilient. As a result, it's very difficult to cause screen burn...but the screen savers look good and are still used.

screen capture

to store the image currently displayed on screen in a file; it is useful when creating manuals about a software product; in Windows, you can capture the current screen to the Clipboard by pressing the PrintScreen key.
see also
PRINT SCREEN

screen dump

printed copy of what is displayed on the screen
see also
PRINT SCREEN

screen font

typeface and size of font used to display text on screen. Windows uses one font to display the names of all the files and folders and window titles. You can change this font setting from the Control Panel/Desktop settings.

screen grab

i) digitizing a single frame from a display or television.
ii) see screen capture

screen saver

software that, after a pre-determined period of inactivity, replaces the existing image on screen and displays moving objects to protect against screen burn. This has now developed into an art form with screen savers often more complex than the applications running on the PC! Flying toasters are a favourite screen saver, although Windows includes a selection of less glamorous screen savers that can be setup and tested in the Control Panel/Desktop settings.
see also
SCREEN BURN

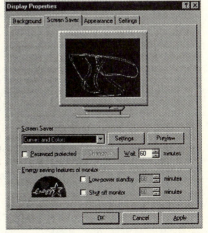

scroll
to move displayed text vertically up or down the screen, one line or pixel at a time

scroll arrows
arrows at the top and bottom of a scroll bar that, when clicked, move the contents of the window up or down or sideways

scroll bar
bar displayed along the side of a window with a marker which indicates how far you have scrolled through the document; by clicking on the scroll arrows at each end of the scoll bar a user can see different parts of the document

Scroll Lock key
key that's rarely used but still included in the top right section of a keyboard; it changes how the cursor control keys operate and is sometimes used in laptops

SCSI
SMALL COMPUTER SYSTEMS INTERFACE
high-speed parallel interface used to connect computers to peripheral devices (such as disk drives and scanners). Fast-SCSI allows data to be transferred at a higher rate than with the original SCSI specification; SCSI-2 is a newer standard that provides a wider data bus and transfers data faster than the original SCSI specification; Wide-SCSI is a development that provides a wider data bus than the original SCSI specification, so can transfer more data at a time; SCSI is the current standard used to interface high-capacity, high-performance disk drives to computers; smaller disk drives are connected with an IDE interface, which is slower, but cheaper. SCSI replaced the older ESDI interface and allows several (normally eight) peripherals to be connected, in a daisy-chain, to one controller

search
function that allows a user to find a word or document in a database or document

search and replace
function in a wordprocessor or database that lets you search for a word or phrase and replace it with something else. In some wordprocessors you can search and replace for formatting or text (for example, replacing all bold text with italic text).

search engine
(on the internet) software that carries out a search of a database when a user asks it to find information; on the internet there are many search engines that list all the Web sites and allow a user to find a Web site by searching for particular information. The big search engines on the internet are Yahoo! (www.yahoo.com), AltaVista (www.digital.altavista.com), InfoSeek (www.infoseek.com)
see also
GOPHER

secondary service provider
organisation that provide internet access for a particular region of a country

sector
smallest area on a magnetic disk which can be addressed by a computer; the disk is divided into concentric tracks, and each track is divided into sectors which, typically, can store 512 bytes of data

secure encryption payment protocol
see
SEPP

secure electronic transactions
see
SET

secure hypertext transfer protocol
see
S-HTTP

secure sockets layer
see
SSL

security
to ensure that your files or computer are protected against unauthorised access make sure that sensitive data or your PC is password protected. Some applications, such as Microsoft Excel, let you password-protect a file. Alternatively, you can set Windows to require a user name and password before it starts. Lastly, you can set a screen-saver to require a password. This is a good idea for the times you nip out for a coffee or lunch break, leaving your PC available to anyone who knows the password. With a password-protected screen saver, you have to enter a password before you can get out of the screen saver and back into Windows.

seek
to move to a particular position in a file or on a disk

seek time
time taken by a read/write head to find a particular track on a disk. Disk drives (and new computers) often state the access and seek times for the drive. The shorter the seek time, the faster the disk drive can move to the correct part of the disk and start reading information.

segment
i) length of cable in a network.
ii) amount of data that is used in a packet sent by a device using the TCP/IP protocol

select
i) to position a pointer over an object (such as a button or menu option) and click on the mouse-button.
ii) to find and retrieve specific information from a database

selection
(in a paint program) to define an area of an image; often used to cut out an area of the image, or to limit a special effect to an area

selection handle
small square displayed on a frame around a selected area that allows the user to change the shape of the area - this is particularly used in drawing and paint programs to let you adjust the shape or size of an object.

selection tool

(in a paint or drawing program), the selection tool is an icon in a toolbar that allows a user to select an area of an image which can then be cut, copied or processed in some way

self extracting archive

compressed file that has includes the program to de-compress the contents; for example, if you download a demonstration program file from the internet, sometimes it is compressed as a ZIP file - you need to use a separate de-compressing utility - or it is supplied as a program file that will automatically de-compress itself when you run it

Send To command

menu command that's available from the File menu of new Windows 95 applications. It allows you to send the file or data currently open in the application to another application, such as an electronic mail system. If you choose the Send To menu option, you can send the document you are working on as an email to another user on the network or you can send it as a fax to a fax machine. The Send To command indicates that the application has been mail-enabled and can interact seamlessly with electronic mail programs.

sensitivity

minimum strength or power of a received signal that is necessary for a microphone to distinguish the signal

SEPP

SECURE ENCRYPTION PAYMENT PROTOCOL

system developed to provide a secure link between a user's browser and a vendor's Web site to allow the user to pay for goods over the internet

see also
PGP, S-HTTP, SSL, STT

sequencer

i) software that allows a user to compose tunes for MIDI instruments, record notes from instruments and mix together multiple tracks.

ii) hardware device that can record or playback a sequence of MIDI notes

serial line internet protocol

see
SLIP

serial port

connector and circuit used to convert the data in a computer to and from a form in which each bit is transmitted one at a time over a single wire. Normally, data in a computer is transferred around the computer in parallel form that is eight or 16 bits wide. If you want to use a modem, you need to send the modem serial data that it can convert into sound signals that can be sent one at a time over a telephone line.

server

dedicated computer which provides a function to a network, such as storing images, or printing data

see also
NETWORK SERVER, WEB SERVER

service provider

company that offers users a connection to the internet; the service provider has a computer that acts as a domain name server and has a high-speed link to the internet, it provides modem access to the internet via point-of-presence telephone numbers. You connect to the internet by setting up an account with the service provider then dialling into its point of presence telephone number with a modem.
see also
ISP

session

i) one or more instances of an application.
ii) (in a PhotoCD) separate occasion when image data is recorded onto a disc

SET
SECURE ELECTRONIC TRANSACTIONS

standards created by a group of banks and internet companies that allow users to buy goods over the internet without risk of hackers; SET provides a secure link between the user's Web browser and the vendor's Web site by encrypting the data transferred
see also
SSL

setup program

utility program that helps you configure your computer or a new software application

SGML
STANDARD GENERAL MARKUP LANGUAGE

method of coding information that is similar to HTML, but includes commands to describe how information is related; normally used to produce multimedia titles rather than for the internet

shadow RAM

method of improving the performance of a PC by copying the contents of a (slow) ROM chip to a faster RAM chip when the computer is first switched on

share-level access

method used to set up network security to protect your local resources. This means that each resource (such as a printer, file or folder) that you want to share with other users on the network can be protected by a password. The alternative to share-level access is called user-level access. Windows for Workgroups and Windows 95 both let you setup share-level access for small networks of two or more PCs that have been connected together.

shared folder

folder of files stored on your computer's local hard disk drive that can be used (or shared) by other users on the network. To share a folder, click once on the folder icon and then click on the right-hand mouse button. Select the Properties option from the pop-up menu and choose Sharing. Once you have set a folder as shareable, the icon for the folder changes so that it now appears with a cable running below the folder to remind you that other users have access to this folder.

shareware

software which is available free to sample, but if kept the user is expected to pay a fee to the writer (often confused with public domain software which is provided completely free of charge)

sheet feed attachment

device which can be attached to a printer to allow single sheets of paper to be fed in automatically

shell

software which operates between the user and the operating system, often to try and make the operating system more friendly or easier to use; for example, MS-DOS's COMMAND.COM is a basic shell that interprets commands typed in at the prompt; Windows 95 is a sophisticated shell with a GUI front-end that's operated by a mouse.

shell out

to temporarily exit from an application to the operating system whilst keeping the original application is still in memory; you can type in operating system commands and then return to the original application by typing the word EXIT.

shielded cable

cable made up of a conductive core surrounded by an insulator, then a conductive layer to protect the transmitted signal against interference and a final outer plastic layer for protection

shielded twisted pair cable (STP)

type of wiring used in Token Ring networks

Shift key

key on a keyboard that, when pressed with another character key will produce an alternative character; for example, the Shift key normally produces an uppercase character or the special character printed on the top part of the key

Shockwave™

system developed by Macromedia that allows Web browsers to display complex multimedia effects

shortcut

feature of Windows 95 that allows a user to define an icon that links to another file or application; for example, you could place shortcut icons on the Windows 95 Desktop to allow you to start an application without using the menu commands. The shortcut has the same icon as the original file but has a tiny arrow in the bottom left-hand corner; the shortcut is not a duplicate of the original, rather it is a pointer to the original file.

shouting

term of abuse that means you are typing a message or article in capital letters; if you submit an article to a newsgroup and the text is entirely in capitals, most other users will assume that you are a new user and do not know that this is disliked

S-HTTP

SECURE HYPERTEXT TRANSFER PROTOCOL

system developed to provide a secure link between a user's browser and a vendor's

Web site to allow the user to pay for goods over the internet
see also
PGP, SEPP, SET, SSL, STT

ShutDown

(in Windows 95) command that will
close down Windows and, if you have a
compatible PC, will switch off the
computer. When you want to switch off
your PC, you should use the ShutDown
command rather than just switch off the
computer since this ensures that all the
files are closed and that Windows sorts
itself out internally before being
switched off. To exit Windows 95

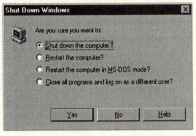

select the Start/ShutDown menu option. With some new PCs, this will also
automatically switch off the PC; with older PCs you need to wait until the screen
tells you it's safe to switch off the PC (which takes around 20 seconds).

SIG
SPECIAL INTEREST GROUP

group of users who have a particular interest and exchange email information or
subscribe to a newsgroup or mailing list

signal

i) generated analog or digital waveform used to carry information.
ii) short message used to carry control codes

signature

i) special authentication code, such as a password, which a user gives prior to
accessing a system or prior to the execution of a task (to prove his identity).
ii) a sentence or paragraph used to end email messages and comments posted on the
internet. Normally a signature should be short - no more than four lines - and might
include a short advertisement for your company and your email address. Most email
programs can add a signature automatically to the end of all email messages you
send.

silicon chip

small piece of silicon in and on the surface of which a complete circuit or logic
function has been produced (by depositing other substances or by doping); silicon is
used in the electronics industry as a base material for integrated circuits. It is grown
as a long crystal which is then sliced into wafers before being etched or treated,
producing several hundred chips per wafer. Other materials, such as germanium or
gallium arsenide, are also used as a base for ICs

silicon disk or RAM disk

area of RAM made to look and behave like a high speed disk drive

SIMM
SINGLE IN-LINE MEMORY MODULE

small, compact circuit board with an edge connector along one edge that carries
densely-packed memory chips, and is used to expand a computer's main memory. If
you want to upgrade your PC by increasing the amount of RAM it has, you can fit
more memory by inserting SIMM cards. Make sure that you buy the correct SIMMs

for your computer - you need to check the type of connector, the speed of the RAM and the capacity of the SIMM or they might not work in your PC. Generally, older PCs, especially 80286 and 80386 use SIMMs with 30-pins, whilst newer 80486 and Pentium-based computers use SIMMs with 72-pins. When buying SIMMs, check whether your computer requires EDO memory, or SIMMs that use an extra parity bit to check the data
see also
DIMM, EDO, PARITY

simple device
multimedia device that does not require a data file for playback, such as a CD drive used to play audio CDs

simple mail transfer protocol
see
SMTP

simple network management protocol
see
SNMP

simulation
computer that is made to imitate a real life situation or a machine, and shows how something works or will work in the future

single in-line memory module
see
SIMM

single speed
speed at which a CD-ROM is spun by a drive - normally 230rpm
see also
DOUBLE SPEED, QUAD SPEED

site
see
WEB SITE

site licence
licence between a software publisher and a user which allows any number of users in one site to use the software

sixteen-bit
processor that handles data in sixteen bit words, providing much faster operation than older eight-bit processors. The Intel 80286 was a sixteen-bit processor that was been replaced by the faster 80386 that could operate on thiry-two bits of data
see also
INTEL, PENTIUM

slave
one device that is controlled by another device

sleep
computer that is waiting for a user to do something! If you have installed power

management on your PC you will find that it shuts down some sections of the computer - such as the hard disk and monitor - after a period of inactivity; these devices will be powered up again as soon as you touch the mouse or hit a key.

SLIP
SERIAL LINE INTERNET PROTOCOL
communications protocol that allows a computer to communicate with the internet via a serial connection (normally a modem and telephone line) rather than a direct network connection; if you connecting to the internet using a modem you will need an account with an ISP or on-line provider - the communications software will dial the access number and establish a SLIP session with the remote computer
see also
ISP, PPP, WINSOCK

slot
see
EXPANSION SLOT

small computer systems interface
see
SCSI

smiley
face created with text characters, used to provide the real meaning to an email message; for example, :-) means laughter or a joke, :-(means sad, ;-) means joke and a wink. Look at this page sideways to see the face

SMT
see
SURFACE-MOUNT TECHNOLOGY

SMTP
SIMPLE MAIL TRANSFER PROTOCOL
standard used to transfer electronic mail messages between computers, normally used to send mail messages from your computer to an internet mail server which can then deliver the message to the correct mail server using SMTP; the destination mail server finally transfers the message to the recipient using POP3 (or sometimes the SMTP) protocol

snail mail
slang term used to refer to the normal (slow) postal delivery rather than (near instant) electronic mail delivery

snd (SouND)
filename extension used to indicate a file that contains digitized sound data
see also
WAV

SNMP
SIMPLE NETWORK MANAGEMENT PROTOCOL
standard set of commands that defines how computers, routers and other communications equipment can be managed from a central location - often used for intranets and large networks

snow
Interference or a fault with a screen that appears as flickering white flecks on the monitor

soak
to run a program or device continuously for a period of time to make sure it functions correctly

socket driver
see
WINSOCK

software
program or group of programs which instructs the hardware on how it should perform, including operating systems, word processors and applications programs

software licence
agreement between a user and a software house, giving details of the rights of the user to use or copy software

software life cycle
period of time when a piece of software exists, from its initial design to the moment when it becomes out of date
see also
VAPOURWARE

software-only video playback
ability to display full-motion video standard that can be played back on any multimedia computer, that does not need special hardware - the decompression and display is carried out by software drivers; any software-only standard does not normally provide as sharp an image as a hardware compression system (such as MPEG) or full-screen playback

solid colour
colour that can be displayed on a screen or printed on a colour printer without dithering
see also
DITHER

solid font printer
printer that uses a whole character shape to print in one movement, such as a daisy wheel printer

solid modelling
function in a graphics program that creates three-dimensional solid-looking objects by shading
see also
RAY-TRACING

sound bandwidth
range of frequencies that a human ear can register, normally from 20Hz to 20KHz

Sound Blaster
type of sound card for PC compatibles developed by Creative Labs that allows sounds to be recorded to disk (using a microphone) and played back; also includes

an FM synthesizer and a MIDI port

sound card
add-on device that plugs into an expansion slot inside your PC and generates analog sound signals. The sound card generates sound from digital data, using either a digital-to-analog converter or a FM synthesis chip; normally also provides functions to record sound in digital form (using an analog-to-digital converter) and control MIDI instruments; unlike Apple Macintosh, PC and compatibles do not come with built-in sound generation hardware, so to produce sound you need to fit a sound card. There are three major standards for PC sound cards: AdLib, SoundBlaster, and Windows-compatible; the MPC Level 1 specification states that a sound card should be able to record sound in 8-bits and sample at 11.025KHz and play back sounds at 11.025KHz and 22.05KHz; the MPC Level 2 specification states that the card should be able to record and play sound files: some sound cards provide built-in compression for wave files, but there are various methods used: the MPC recommends ADCPM. In addition, many PC sound cards include electronics to generate sounds from MIDI data on-board: there are two kinds of MIDI sound generation: FM synthesis simulates musical notes by modulating the frequency of a base carrier wave, whereas waveform synthesis uses digitized samples of the notes to produce a more realistic sound
see also
ADPCM; MIDI; SAMPLE RATE; SAMPLE SIZE

sound file
file stored on disk that contains sound data; this can either be a digitized analog sound signal or notes for a MIDI instrument

Sound Recorder
utility included with Microsoft Windows that allows a user to playback digitzed sound files (the .WAV standard) or record sound onto disk and carry out very basic editing once you have recorded the sound.

sound waves
pressure waves produced by vibrations, which are transmitted through air (or a solid) and detected by the human ear or a microphone (in which they are converted to electrical signals)

source file
(in Windows) the file that contains the data referenced by an OLE object; for example, if you have an OLE object with a link to a spreadsheet, the spreadsheet file is the source file
see also
OLE

source object
(in Windows) within a drag and drop operation the source object is the object that is first clicked on and then dragged

spam
slang term that refers to an article that has been posted to more than one newsgroup, so is likely to contain commercial messages; newsgroup users do not like spammed messages or spamming and will flame users that submit this type of article

special interest group
see
SIG

speech recognition
analysis of spoken words in such a way that a computer can recognize spoken words and commands

speech synthesis
to produce spoken words by a sound card or speech synthesizer
see also
PHONEME

spellcheck
function of wordprocessors and DTP programs that can check the spelling of words in a document by comparing them with an exisitng dictionary file; the spellcheck function can sometimes include a thesaurus that will display similar words to the mis-spelt word or a sound-like function (called soundex) that displays words that sound the same but have different spellings.

spike
very short electrical pulse that can cause damage to electronic equipment

splash screen
initial screen that's displayed for a few seconds when you start a program. The splash screen normally displays the product logo and gives basic copyright information.

spool
to store documents in a queue before they are printed
see also
PRINT QUEUE

split screen
to divide the display screen of an application into two or more sections that you can then modify independently. For example, in Word for Windows, you can open several documents at the same time and arrange the screen so that it is divided to display all the documents at the same time.

SPX
SEQUENCED PACKET EXCHANGE
protocol used by the Novell NetWare network operating system to guarantee that information transferred over a local area network arrives correctly; the SPX protocol uses the Novell IPX protocol to actually transfer the data, but ensures delivery
see also
IPX, NETBIOS

SRAM
see
STATIC RAM

SSL
SECURE SOCKETS LAYER
protocol designed by Netscape that provides secure communications over the

internet; normally used to protect a user when sending credit card or other payment details over the internet. To provide a secure communications link, the user needs to have a Web browser that can support SSL (such as the Netscape Navigator browser) and the company selling goods needs an internet server that provides SSL feature. When the user connects to the secure Web server, the browser automatically recognises that SSL is available and provides a secure link that encrypts any information before sending it over the telephone line. You can see if a secure SSL link has been established by the status of the small key icon in the bottom left-hand corner of the Netscape Navigator screen: if the key is broken, there is no secure link, if the key is solid there is a secure link
see also
PGP, SEPP, SET, STT

stack
area of memory that is used to store data when a software program is being run; the stack is setup and managed automatically by the software

stack overflow
error message that is sometimes displayed - if you see this error message when running an application it means that there is not enough free memory on your computer for the program's needs and is normally caused by poor programming; you should contact the software publisher

standard memory
first 1Mb of memory in a PC
see also
EXPANDED MEMORY, UPPER MEMORY

standard mode
(in an IBM PC) mode of operation of Microsoft Windows which uses extended memory but does not allow multitasking of DOS applications

star topology
network configuration in which all nodes (computers or printers) are connected to a central device, called the hub, that ensures that data is correctly transferred from one node to another

Start button
button that's normally in the bottom left-hand corner of a Windows 95 Desktop screen. The Start button provides a convenient route to the programs and files on your computer. Initially, the Start button has categories for Programs, Accessories, Settings and recently accessed documents. However, you can also add you own applications to the Start menu by moving the pointer over the Start button and clicking on the right-hand mouse button. A second tip, the Start button is at the very left of the taskbar in Windows 95. You can move the entire taskbar to any of the four sides of the screen by clicking on the bar and dragging it to another edge.

startup disk
floppy disk which holds the operating system and system configuration files which can, in case of hard disk failure, be used to boot the computer

Startup folder
special folder on your hard disk that contains programs that will be run automatically when you next start Windows. If you want to run a diary or calendar

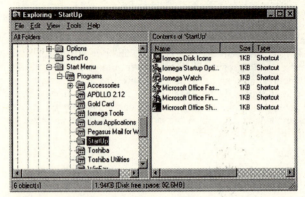

Startup folder within Windows 95

program each time you start Windows, move the program icon into the Startup folder.

startup screen

text or graphics displayed when an application or multimedia book is run; normally displays the product name, logo and copyright information and is only displayed for a few seconds before the main screen appears

see also
SPLASH SCREEN

static electricity

electrical charge that can build up in a person or electronic component; in a person, static electricity often builds up after walking on carpets and can seriously damage electronic components if you discharge the electricity by touching a computer

static RAM (SRAM)

RAM that retains data for as long as the power supply is on, and does not require the data to be refreshed; static RAM requires less electrical power than dynamic RAM components and is normally faster, but costs more - it is often used for specialised functions where speed is important, such as in cache memory

see also
RAM, REFRESH

status bar

line at the top or bottom of a screen which gives information about the task currently being worked on (position of cursor, number of lines, filename, time, etc.)

stereo or stereophonic

sound recorded onto two separate channels from two separate microphone elements and played back through a pair of headphones or two speakers; each channel is slightly different to give the impression that the sound is live rather than recorded, and has depth

stick model

see
WIRE FRAME

stop bit

information transmitted at the end of section of data to indicate to the receiver that this is the end of the data; normally used when sending data over an asynchronous serial link to indicate the end of each byte or character of data

store-and-forward
basic method of transferring mail by moving a copy of the message to another server on its way between the sender and the recipient
see also
MHS

story board
series of pictures or drawings that show how a video or animation progresses

STP
see
SHIELDED TWISTED PAIR

string
series of consecutive alphanumeric characters or words that are manipulated and treated as a single unit by the computer

stroke
i) the width (in pixels) of the pen or brush used to draw on-screen.
ii) the thickness of a printed character

STT
SECURE TRANSACTION TECHNOLOGY
system developed to provide a secure link between a user's browser and a vendor's Web site to allow the user to pay for goods over the internet
see also
PGP, SEPP, SET, S-HTTP, SSL

style
typeface, font, point size, colour, spacing and margins of text in a formatted document

style sheet
template which can be preformatted to automatically set the style or layout of a document such as a manual, a book, a newsletter, etc. The style sheet includes margins, fonts and type-styles used for different paragraphs

subdirectory
directory of disk or tape contents contained within another directory

sub-domain
second level of addressing on the internet that normally refers to a department name within a larger organisation

submenu
secondary menu displayed as a choice from a menu; used if there are too many choices to fit into one menu. A good example is the Start button menu which has several submenus for the Program and Settings menu option.

subscribe
to add your name to a mailing list or listserv list so that you will receive any messages for the group; to subscribe to a list you normally send your name and

email address to the manager of the list, but you should check beforehand. One of the best ways of finding out how to subscribe is to look at the www.liszt.com Web site that lists every mailing list and tells you how to subscribe
see also
LISTSERV, MAILING LIST

subscript
small character which is printed below the line of other characters

sub-woofer
large loudspeaker that can reproduce very low frequency sounds (normally with frequencies between 20 to 100Hz) that is used with normal loudspeakers to enhance the overall sound quality

Sun Microsystems™
company that developed the Java programming system used to extend Web pages

supercomputer
very powerful mainframe computer used for high speed mathematical or imaging tasks

superscript
small character printed above the normal line of characters

super VGA
see
SVGA

surf
to explore a web site looking at the web pages in no particular order, but simply moving between pages using the links; normally used to mean exploring web pages for pleasure with no particular reason

surface-mount technology (SMT)
method of manufacturing circuit boards in which the electronic components are bonded directly onto the surface of the board rather than being inserted into holes and soldered into place. Newer PCs and peripherals are now constructed with surface-mount technology which is cheaper and more reliable than the older method of using sockets. The only exception is memory (which is normally fitted in SIMM cards - themselves using surface-mount technology) and the processor which is normally fitted in a ZIF socket.

surge
sudden increase in electrical power in a system, due to a fault or noise or component failure

surge protector
electrical device (normally part of a power supply unit in a computer) that is used to protect electronic equipment against damage caused by a surge

suspend
command that is used when running Windows 95 on a battery-powered laptop computer to shut down almost all of the electronic components of the laptop, but to provide enough electrical power to the main memory so that it retains all the data and programs that you were running; after you have suspended the laptop you can

switch the laptop on again and instantly resume work where you were. If you do not use the suspend mode and instead switch the laptop off, all power is cut off and, when you switch the laptop on again it will have to boot up and you will need to start the applications again

SVGA
SUPER VGA
enhancement to the standard VGA graphics display system which allows resolutions of up to 800x600pixels with 16million colours

swap
to stop using one program, put it and its data into store temporarily, run another program, and when that is finished, return to the first one

swap file
file stored on the hard disk used as a temporary storage area for data held in RAM, to provide virtual memory
see also
PERMANENT SWAP FILE, VIRTUAL MEMORY

switch
extra options that are added after the main command that is typed in at the command line; for example, if you type in DIR at the DOS prompt, you will see a list of the files stored on your computer; if you add the switch '/p' and type in 'DIR /P' the list of files will pause after each page

SX
type of processor chip derived from the basic 80386 or 80486 processor that is slightly cheaper to manufacturer and buy; the 80386-SX does not have a floating point processor and only supports a 16-bit internal data path, the 80486-SX does not have a floating point processor

Symbol font
TrueType font that's included with Windows and includes all sorts of symbols and Greek characters
see also
TRUETYPE

synchronous cache
high-speed secondary cache system used in many computers that use the Pentium processor chip
see also
SECONDARY CACHE

synchronous DRAM
new high-speed memory technology in which the memory components work from the same clock signal as the main processor, so are synchronized. This allows data to be transferred between the memory and processor without using special commands to check that the data transfer has been carried out correctly, so improving the performance

synchronous transmission
data transmission at a fixed speed and in which the transmitter and receiver are synchronized so that no extra timing signal is required. Normally used by

mainframe or high-speed computers to transfer data to another device
see also
AUTOSYNC

system
general term that refers to a computer or to a computer and its associated
peripherals or to the operating system software (such as Windows)

System 7™
operating system software used on an Apple Macintosh computer

system administrator
see
NETWORK ADMINISTRATOR

system backup
copy of all the data stored on a computer, server or network. The system can be a
single computer or could be a network of computers.

system board
see
MOTHERBOARD

system clock
electronic component that generates a regular signal that is used to synchronize all
the components in the computer

system colours
palette of 20 colours that are used by Windows for colouring window elements such
as borders, captions, buttons

system disk
disk which holds the system software that is used to boot up a computer and load
the operating system ready for use. Most PCs have the operating system software
stored on the internal hard disk.

System Monitor
utility provided with Windows 95 that allows you to view how the resources on
your PC are performing and, if you have shared the device, who else on the network
is using them.

system software
software which makes everything in your computer work correctly. The system
software controls the hardware and manages programs. It looks after and controls
all aspects of the computer; Windows 95 is a form of system software, since it
operates everything itself and does not rely on other software. This is different from
Windows 3.1x which relied on MS-DOS to manage the hardware; in this latter case
MS-DOS is the system software. In both cases, the useful software that a user
would use - such as a wordprocessor - is called the application software.

system unit
main box of a personal computer that contains the motherboard and hard disk drive

Tt

T1

(US term) for a leased line connection that transfers data at 1.544Mbits per second and can carry either data or 24 voice channels; if the link uses only part of this capacity, it is called a fractional T1 link. These links are normally used to connect ISPs together or to connect offices of a large organisation

see also
LEASED LINE

tab

i) to tabulate or to arrange text in columns with the cursor automatically running from one column to the next in keyboarding.

ii) in Windows, a method of moving from one button or field to another without using the mouse, but by pressing the tab key to move the focus

tabbing order

order in which the focus moves from one button or field to the next as the user presses the tab key

tab key

key on a keyboard, normally positioned on the far left, beside the 'Q' key, with two arrows pointing in opposite horizontal directions, used to insert a tab character into text and so align the text at a preset tab stop

table

HTML command that allows a Web page designer to display text or other information within a series of columns and rows on a Web page; tables are often used to create a basic layout for a Web page as well as to display information in a tabular format (such as a price list or catalogue)

for a complete list of HTML commands, see
APPENDIX

tab rack

graduated scale, displayed along the top of the screen, showing the position of tabulation columns

tab settings *or* tab stops

preset points where the cursor will stop each time the tab key is pressed

table of contents

i) (in a CD) data at the start of the disc that describes how many tracks are on the CD, their position and length.

ii) (in a multimedia title) page with a list of the headings of all the other main pages in the title and links so that a user can move to them

tag

word or letters within HTML that carries out a function; for example, the tag <b>
will format the text as bold, the tag <hr> will display a horizontal line
for a complete list of HTML tags, see
APPENDIX

tag image file format

see
TIFF

tape backup

high-capacity storage device that uses a tape cartridge or tape cassette to hold a
large amount of data; normally used to create a backup copy of the information
stored on a hard disk

tar

TAPE ARCHIVE
file compression system used on a computer running the Unix operating system

taskbar

bar that normally runs along the bottom of the screen in Windows 95 and displays
the Start button and a list of other programs or windows that are currently active.
You can move the entire taskbar to any of the four sides of the screen by clicking on
the bar and dragging it to another edge.

TCP/IP

TRANSMISSION CONTROL PROTOCOL / INTERNET PROTOCOL
set of communications protocols developed by the US Department of Defense
(DOD), originally for use in military applications. TCP/IP bundles and unbundles
sent and received data into packets, manages packet transmission and checks for
errors across networks. Originally found binding Unix networks together, its
flexibility and portability are making it a de facto standard for any LAN and WAN.
It is most often encountered as the set of standard commands used in networks and
in the internet to allow computers to exchange information.

technical support

person who provides technical advice to a user to explain how to use software or
hardware or explain why it might not work

telecommuting

practice of working on a computer in one place (normally from home) that is linked
by modem to the company's central office allowing messages and data to be
transferred

teleconferencing

to link video, audio and computer signals from different locations so that distant
people can talk and see each other, as if in a conference room

telephony

series of standards that define the way in which computers can work with a
telephone system to provide voice-mail, telephone answering, and fax services

telnet

software that allows you to connect to and control via the internet a remote computer as if you were there and type in commands as if you were sitting in front of the computer. In practice, Telnet is normally used when you are setting up your Web site to create directories, set up security and move files.

template
(in a wordprocessor) file containing standard section of text (such as a memo or invoice) into which specific details (company address or prices or quantities) can be added
see also
STYLE SHEET

10Base-T
cabling and connection standard used to carry Ethernet signals. 10BaseT is the offspring of the generic Ethernet specification which defines data transmission of 10Mbits per second using 802.3 data packets over twisted pair cable with telephone-style RJ-45 connectors. Unlike Thin-Wire Ethernet, 10Base-T has a physical star topology that makes it more robust and more secure than its predecessor. However, it needs a central hub

Terminal
simple communications program that is supplied with Windows 3.1x (Windows 95 includes the similar HyperTerminal program) and can be used to connect to bulletin boards but cannot connect directly to the internet.

terminal emulation software
software program that is used to allow a computer to interpret the special display codes used to control a specialist workstation; normally used with a modem to allow you to connect to a remote mainframe computer system

terminate and stay resident (TSR) program
program which loads itself into main memory and carries out a function when activated, normally by a special key sequence or an instruction; used for utilities and for drivers (such as a CD-ROM driver)

terminator
small connector that includes a resistor that fits onto the last SCSI device in your computer. SCSI devices, such as CD-ROM drives or scanners, are connected in a one after another (in daisy-chain fashion) and the terminator is fitted to the last SCSI device to create a complete electrical circuit

text file
file stored on disk that contains text rather than graphics or data; the text is not formatted or laid out in any way and the file contains no font or typeface information; to edit a text file you can the EDIT utility from the MS-DOS prompt, or the NotePad utility in Windows; alternatively, you can use any wordprocessor that can save to an ASCII or text file format

text mode
operating mode of a computer or display screen that will only display pre-defined characters and will not allow graphic images to be displayed; Windows operates in a graphics mode, MS-DOS normally operates in a text mode

texture mapping
i) special computer graphics effect using algorithms to produce an image that looks

like the surface of something (such as marble, brick, stone or water).
ii) to cover one image with another to give the first a texture; for example, if you
have an image of a house, you could cover it with an image of a brick and the result
is a house filled with a brick pattern

TFT screen
THIN FILM TRANSISTOR SCREEN
method of creating a high-quality colour LCD display used in laptop computers. A
TFT screen can display very clear, bright and sharp images with tens of thousands
of different colours but are more expensive to manufacture and require more
electrical power.

thesaurus
file that contains synonyms that are displayed as alternatives to a misspelt word
during a spellcheck

thin film transistor screen
see
TFT SCREEN

thirty-two bit system (32-bit)
processor that handles data in thirty-two bit words
see
PROCESSOR

thrashing
i) excessive disk activity.
ii) configuration or program fault in a virtual memory system, that results in a CPU
wasting time moving pages of data between main memory and disk or backing store

thread
series of related messages or replies to an original message within a discussion
group or newsgroup; most newsreader programs will organise threads of messages
so that you can read them together

threshold
preset level which causes an action if a signal exceeds or drops below it; for
example, if using a microphone in a noisy environment you might set the threshold
high so that only loud noises are recorded

thumbnail
miniature graphical representation of an image; used as a quick and convenient
method of viewing the contents of graphics or DTP files before they are retrieved

TIFF
TAG IMAGE FILE FORMAT
file format used to store graphic images (developed by Aldus and Microsoft) that
can handle monochrome, grey-scale, 8-bit or 24-bit colour images; there have been
many different versions of TIFF that include several different compression
algorithms

time out
i) connection closed because a response has not been received within the time

expected.

ii) feature of communications software that will cut the modem connection if you do not type anything for a period of time

tile

to arrange a group of windows so that they are displayed side by side without overlapping

title bar

horizontal bar at the top of a window which displays the title of the window or application

token

special code used in some network systems (particularly the Token Ring network system) that are used to control which computer can transmit information onto the network

Token Ring network

network system developed by IBM; the nodes of the network (computers and printers) are connected together in a loop

compare with
ETHERNET

toner

finely powdered ink (usually black) that is used in laser printers; the toner is transferred onto the paper by electrical charge, then fixed permanently to the paper by heating. As a tip, if you spill toner onto your clothes or hands when changing a toner cartridge, wash off with cold water. If you wash the toner with hot water, this will fix it permanently to your hands or clothes!

toner cartridge

plastic container that holds powdered toner for use in a laser printer

toolbar

window that contains a range of icons that access tools; for example, paint programs normally have a toolbar that includes icons for colour, brush, circle, and eraser tools; a floating toolbar is a moveable window that can be positioned anywhere on screen

ToolTips

feature of applications that work under Windows that display a
line of descriptive text under an icon when you move the pointer
over the icon.

topology

arrangement of connections within a network; for example, a ring topology means that all the nodes of the network are connected to form a closed loop; in a star topology each node is connected to a central hub and in a bus topology each node is connected to a long cable that has a terminator at each end

touch pad

flat device which can sense where on its surface and when it is touched, used to control the cursor position. Touch pads are now fitted to some laptops instead of a trackball or mouse as a way of controlling Windows.

touch screen
computer display which has a grid of infrared transmitters and receivers, positioned on either side of the screen, used to control a cursor position (when a user wants to make a selection or move the cursor, he points to the screen, breaking two of the beams, which gives the position of his finger)

tracing
function of a graphics program that takes a bitmap image and processes it to find the edges of the shapes and so convert these into a vector line image that can be more easily manipulated

track
i) (in a music CD) a song.
ii) (in a MIDI file) method of separating the notes within a tune either by channel or by part or instrument.
iii) (in multimedia authoring software) series of instructions that define how an object moves with time

trackball
device used to move a cursor on-screen, which is controlled by turning a ball contained in a case with the palm of your hand; rather similar to a mechanical mouse turned up-side down

tracking
see
MOUSE TRACKING

traffic
data that is being transmitted over a network or communications link

Transmission Control Protocol / internet Protocol
see
TCP/IP

transputer
single, large, very powerful processor that can be connected in parallel to other similar processors and which effectively multiplies the processing power.

tree of folders
view of all the folders stored on your disk arranged to show folders and sub-folders.

TrueType
outline font technology introduced by Apple and Microsoft as a means of printing exactly what is displayed on screen and providing fonts that can be scaled to any point size whilst still being smooth
see also
OUTLINE FONT

TSR
TERMINATE AND STAY RESIDENT (PROGRAM)

tunnelling
method of enclosing a packet of data from one type of network within another

packet so that it can be sent over a different, incompatible, network

tweening

see
MORPHING

twisted pair

network cable that is made by twisting together two thin insulated wires, this type of cable is much cheaper and easier to handle than coaxial cable and the twisting helps to cut down interference from other electrical equipment; twisted pair cable is normally used with 10Base-T networking equipment

compare with
COAXIAL

type size

size of a font, measured in points

type style

weight and angle of a font, such as bold or italic

typeface

set of characters in a particular design and particular weight

Uu

UART

UNIVERSAL ASYNCHRONOUS RECEIVER/TRANSMITTER

circuit that converts between the parallel data used by PCs and the serial data used by modems. Serial ports have a UART, while internal modems supply their own. For high DTE rates on systems with a heavy processing load (typically those that use Windows), a 16550A UART provides better, more reliable performance.

undelete

function of Windows and DOS that lets you restore deleted information or a deleted file; in DOS you can type Undelete and DOS will attempt to recover your file. If you have mistakenly deleted a file, do not save any other files onto the disk, but run the undelete command immediately. In Windows 95, you can retrieve the file from the Recycle Bin: double-click on the Recycle bin icon on the Desktop to see a list of files that can be undeleted.

underline or underscore

i) line drawn or printed under a piece of text.

ii) to draw a line under a piece of text

undo

function of some wordprocessors and other applications that will let you undo the command you've just carried out - for example it can undo a paste or a delete operation. Microsoft applications have now standardised on Ctrl-Z as the keyboard shortcut to undo the last action

uniform resource locator

see
URL

uninterruptable power supply

see
UPS

Unix

multiuser, multitasking operating system developed by AT&T Bell Laboratories to run on almost any computer, from a PC to minicomputers and large mainframes; there are a number of graphical user interfaces, such as Open Look, that hide the Unix command-line; Unix is the operating system that is normally used to run Web server software, such as Apache

unmoderated list

mailing list that sends any material submitted to the listserv on to all the subscribers without a person reading or checking the content
see also
MAILING LIST, LISTSERV

upgrade

to improve the performance or specification of your computer by adding more RAM, a bigger hard disk or some other improvement.

upload

to send a file from your computer to the hard disk of another computer, particularly used to refer to sending files over the internet to another server
compare
DOWNLOAD

upper memory

(in an IBM PC) 384Kb of memory located between the 640Kb and 1Mb limits; upper memory is located after the 640Kb conventional memory, before the high memory areas above the 1Mb range

UPS

UNINTERRUPTABLE POWER SUPPLY
electrical device that will supply electrical power to a computer if the mains power is cut off; a UPS normally works from a battery and gives the user a few extra minutes in which to save data files and shutdown the computer

URL

UNIFORM RESOURCE LOCATOR
(internet) system used to standardize the way in which WWW addresses are written; for example, the URL of the Peter Collin Publishing home page is 'http://www.pcp.co.uk'. A DNS server looks up the URL in a table that provides the unique numerical address for this WWW page
see also
DNS

usability

measure of the ease with which hardware or software can be used

Usenet

section of the internet that provides forums (called newsgroups) in which any user can add a message or comment on any other message; often the busiest part of the internet
see also
NEWSGROUPS

user-friendly

software that is easy to use and interact with

user interface

part of the software that a user sees and works with; often refers to the operating system features that make the operating system more friendly or easier to use; for example, MS-DOS is a basic shell that interprets commands typed in at the prompt;

the Microsoft Windows is a graphical user interface that is easier to use
see also
GUI

Uuencoding

method of converting documents and files to a pseudo-text format that allows you to transmit them as an electronic mail message. This gets around the internet's inability to transfer messages that are not text. Now been largely replaced by MIME

Vv

V.29
standard for transmitting facsimile data under the international Group 3 FAX standard. Its maximum transmission speed is 9,600 bps.

V.32
communications standard defined by the CCITT that defines data transmission using a modem in which the data-transmission rate is 9,600 bps.

V.32bis
communications standard defined by the CCITT that defines data transmission using a modem in which the data transmission at 14,400 bps and several slower rates.

V.32terbo
pseudo-standard developed by AT&T, among others, that supports transmission at 19,200 bps. The name is a phonetic play on words - officially, the next revision after V.32bis would be called V.32ter.

V.42
communications standard defined by the CCITT that defines error control when transmitting data using a modem; the standard is based on a European error-control standard called LAP M, which also can use MNP Classes 2-4.

V.42bis
communications standard defined by the CCITT that defines data compression when transmitting data using a modem; the standard requires V.42. Under ideal conditions, V.42bis can provide up to fourfold compression.

vapourware
products which exist in name only

VB
see
VISUAL BASIC

VBA
VISUAL BASIC FOR APPLICATIONS
complex macro language developed by Microsoft from its Visual Basic programming tool. Now, almost all Microsoft applications, including Word, Excel and Access can use macros written in the VBA language providing a very powerful macro language

VBScript™

set of programming commands that can be included within a normal Web page (that is written using HTML commands); the VBScript commands carry out a function to enhance the Web page - such as providing the time of day, animation or form processing. An ActiveX applet is a self-contained program file that is downloaded separately from the Web page and run on the user's computer; a VBScript program is a series of commands included within a Web page HTML file and executed by the Web browser. To write VBScript you need to learn the script commands and then use an editor to add them into your Web page file; to create an ActiveX application you need a program compiler and programming skills
see also
ACTIVEX APPLET, JAVA, JAVASCRIPT

vector font

shape of characters within a font that are drawn using curves and lines (vector graphics) allowing the characters to be scaled to almost any size without changing the quality
compare with
BIT-MAPPED FONT

vector graphics or vector image or vector scan

system of drawing objects using curves and lines. The images are described by line length and direction from an origin to plot lines and so build up an image rather than a description of each pixel, as in a bitmap; a vector image can be easily and accurately re-sized with no loss of detail
compare with
BITMAP IMAGE

vendor-independent messaging

see
VIM

Veronica

tool that works with Gopher to help a user find information or files on the WWW
see also
GOPHER

vertical application

program that has been designed for a specific use, rather than for general use. For example, a wordprocessor is a general use program whereas software to run a betting shop is a vertical application

vertical justification

adjustment of the spacing between lines of text to fit a section of text into the height of a page

VESA local bus (VL-bus)

VIDEO ELECTRONICS STANDARDS ASSOCIATION
standard defined by VESA that provides a high-speed local bus that runs at 40 or 60MHz and transfers parallel data 32-bits or 64-bits at a time. The system is most often used in Pentium-based personal computers for network or graphics adapters. This high-speed connection on the motherboard of your PC can be used by components that need to exchange large amounts of information at high speed

without interrupting the main processor, so improving performance
compare with
PCI

VFW
see
VIDEO FOR WINDOWS

VGA
VIDEO GRAPHICS ARRAY
(in an IBM PC) standard of video adapter developed by IBM that can support a display with a resolution up to 640x480 pixels in up to 256 colours; superseded by SVGA which is an enhancement to the standard VGA graphics display system that allows resolutions of up to 800x600pixels with 16 million colours

VGA feature connector
26-pin edge connector or port (normally at the top edge) of a VGA display adapter that allows another device to access its palette information and clock signals; often used to provide overlays; for example, a board that displays TV images in a window on screen needs to be synchronized with the VGA adapter

video adapter or board or controller
board that plugs into an expansion socket inside your PC and converts data into electrical signals to drive a monitor and display text and graphics

video capture board
board that plugs into an expansion socket inside your PC and lets you capture a TV picture and store it in memory so that it can then be processed by a computer

video conference
to link two or more computers that can capture and display video and audio in real time so that distant people can talk and see each other, as if in a conference room

video digitizer
high speed digital sampling circuit which stores a TV picture in memory so that it can then be processed by a computer

videodisc
read-only optical disc that can store up to two hours of video data; normally used either to store a complete film (as a rival to video cassette) or to use in an interactive system with text, video and still images - for interactive use, a videodisc can store 54,000 frames of information. NOTE: if the videodisc contains a complete film, the data is recorded using a constant linear velocity format; if used to store interactive data, it is stored in a constant angular velocity format

Video Electronics Standards Association
see
VESA

Video for Windows™ (VFW)
set of software drivers and utilities for Microsoft Windows 3.1, developed by Microsoft, that allows AVI-format video files to be played back in a window; Video for Windows supports several different compression methods including Microsoft Video 1, Microsoft RLE and Intel's Indeo. Once the Video for Windows driver is

installed, Video clips can be played back using the Windows Media Player utility; sequences can be edited using the supplied VidEdit utility and video recorded with the VidCap utility; the quality of the video playback depends on the performance of the PC hardware, and the size of the playback window. With a window size of 160x120 pixels, any 486 or higher processor can display flicker-free video; for full-screen video playback at 640x480 pixels only a Pentium-based PC can display smooth motion

video game
game played on a computer that can be either an adventure game where you have to explore an electronic world or an arcade game in which you have to outwit or shoot lots of baddies!

video graphics array
see
VGA

video graphics card or overlay card
expansion card that fits into an expansion slot inside your PC and that allows a computer to display both generated text and graphics and moving video images from an external camera or VCR

video memory or video RAM (VRAM)
section of memory fitted on a video adapter that is used as a temporary store for image data sent from the computer's main memory or to store an image as it is built up and before it is displayed on the screen

VIM
VENDOR-INDEPENDENT MESSAGING
set of standards developed by IBM, Borland, Novell and Apple, that provides a way of sending electronic mail messages between applications
compare with
MAPI

virtual
something that does not actually exist, except in an imaginary form in a computer

virtual address
address that refers to a location in vitual memory

virtual desktop or screen
area that is bigger than the physical limits of the monitor, and which can contain text, images, windows, etc; the monitor acts as a window onto this area and a user can scroll around to view a different parts of the virtual screen; often used to help organise a window that has lots of icons

virtual image
complete image stored in memory rather than the part of it that is displayed

virtual memory
large, imaginary, main memory made available to an operating system by storing unused parts of the virtual memory on disk and then transferring these pages into

available main memory as and when they are required

virtual reality (VR)
simulation of a real-life scene or environment by a computer with which you can interact and explore

virtual reality modeling language
see
VRML

virus
software that is designed to corrupt your data files and copy itself automatically from one computer to another, usually by attaching itself to a normal application file; if you download a lot of programs from the internet, you should carry out a regular check with a virus checker that your computer has not been infected by a virus

virus checker
software that is used to try and detect and remove unwanted virus programs from the hard disk of your computer

Visual Basic™
programming tool developed by Microsoft, that allows users to create Windows applications very easily. Visual Basic is a rapid application development (RAD) tool that allows users with little programming knowledge to create a complex Windows application - although the finished applications are not as fast as programs written in C

Visual Basic Script™
see
VBSCRIPT

Visual Basic for Applications™ (VBA)
see
VBA

VL-bus or VL local bus
see
VESA

voice
i) (in MIDI) another name for a note or sound effect (such as a whistle); instruments that are multi-voice can play several notes at the same time.
ii) sound of a person speaking

voice mail
sophisticated telephone answering machine normally used in large companies, but also a feature of some new modems

volatile
electronic memory component that does not retain information when the electrical power is switched off

volume
convenient name used to identify a particular hard disk, CD-ROM drive or tape unit

within a computer; if you are using a very large hard disk you can split it into several volumes to help organise your files

volume label
name given to a hard disk using the VOL command from MS-DOS or by selecting the Properties page of the disk within Windows 95

VR
see
VIRTUAL REALITY

VRAM
see
VIDEO RAM

VRML
VIRTUAL REALITY MODELING LANGUAGE
system that allows developers to create three-dimensional worlds within a Web page; a user can move through the three-dimensional world to see shops, products, and shapes in shaded three-dimensions. This system provides a way of allowing the user to explore a Web site by moving through the landscape rather than viewing fixed, two-dimensional images. In order to view a Web site that uses VRML you will need a Web browser with a VRML 3-D plug-in extension. Netscape currently use a VRML system called Live3D, Microsoft use ActiveVRML
see also
PLUG-IN

Ww

WAIS
WIDE AREA INFORMATION SERVER
system that allows a user to search for information stored on the internet
see also
ARCHIE, GOPHER, SEARCH INDEX

wait state
delay that is introduced to allow a fast central processor to store or retrieve data from slower memory components

wallpaper
(in Microsoft Windows) image or pattern used as a background in a window. You can change the background colour or image displayed by Windows from within the Control Panel/Desktop icon settings.

WAN
WIDE AREA NETWORK
many small, linked local area networks or a network with multiple servers linked together using public telephone circuits, leased lines or high-speed bridges.

warm boot
reset operation that will load the operating system, but does not clear all of the computer's memory; if your computer stops working correctly you might have to carry out a warm boot by pressing the Ctrl-Alt-Del keys together
see also
RESET

WAV file
see
WAVE

WAVE or WAV file
standard method of storing an analog signal in digital form under Microsoft Windows (files have the .WAV extension)

wavetable
memory in a sound card that contains a recording of a real musical instrument that is played back; this method of producing sounds is different from an FM synthesis sound card that generates the sound using mathematical equations

WebBot™
utility used in Microsoft internet software that helps a user create a particular

function in a Web page; for example, a WebBot can create a catalogue request form or can create a table for information. Instead of using complex HTML commands, you can enter the information into the WebBot and it will create the elements. If you want to use WebBots in your Web page, your Web server must support the WebBot extensions - check with your ISP

Web browser
see
BROWSER

Web crawler
software that moves over every new Web page on the internet and produces an index based on the content of the Web pages - normally used by search engines to ensure that they are up to date

Web page
single file stored on a Web server that contains formatted text, graphics and hypertext links to other pages on the internet. A Web page is created using HTML codes and is viewed with a browser
see
BROWSER, HTML, APPENDIX A

Web server
computer that stores the collection of Web pages that make up a Web site

what you see is what you get (WYSIWYG)
wordprocessing or DTP program where what you see on the screen is exactly the same as the image or text that will be printed, including graphics and special fonts

white pages
database of users and their email address stored on the internet to help other users find an email address; normally you have to add your own email address to the database

wide area information server
see
WAIS

wide area network
see
WAN

wild card character
symbol used when searching for files or data which represents all files; in DOS, UNIX and PC operating systems, the wild card character '?' will match any single character in this position; the wild card character 'or' means match any number of any characters
see also
QUESTION MARK

window
i) reserved section of screen used to display special information, that can be selected and looked at at any time and which overwrites information already on the screen.

ii) part of a document currently displayed on a screen.

iii) area of memory or access to a storage device

Windows
multitasking graphical user interface for the IBM PC developed by Microsoft Corp. that is designed to be easy to use; Windows uses icons to represent files and devices and can be controlled using a mouse, unlike MS-DOS which requires commands to be typed in

Windows 3.1
first of the new generation of Windows which provided features including OLE and drag and drop.

Windows 3.11™
see
WINDOWS FOR WORKGROUPS

Windows 3.1x
refers to any version of Windows after version 3, including 3.1 and 3.11

Windows 95™
current version of Microsoft's Windows that provides support for long filenames, an interface that's easier to use and better support for networks and the internet. It does, however, require a faster processor and more memory to get good results - an absolute minimum of 8Mb and a fast 80486 processor are required.

Windows CE™
software operating system developed by Microsoft and designed to run on small PDA or palmtop computers that use either a pen input or a keyboard instead of a mouse; this version looks like and can run similar applications to Windows 95

Windows Explorer™
software utility included with Windows 95 that lets you view the folders and files on your hard disk, floppy disk, CD-ROM and any shared network drives.

Windows for Workgroups™
version of Microsoft's Windows that includes the functions that let you connect several computers together to form a network and share files, printers and exchange data. It also includes software for email, fax and scheduler utilities

Windows NT™
high-performance operating system derived from Microsoft's Windows that provides a robust, fast operating system for network workstations or for the central server in a network

Winsock
utility software that is required to control the modem when connecting to the internet under MS-DOS or Windows 3 and allows the computer to communicate using the TCP/IP protocol. Windows 95 has its own version of this utility built in.

wire frame model
(in graphics and CAD) objects displayed using lines and arcs rather than filled areas or having the appearance of being solid

wizard

software utility that helps you create something; for example, if you want to design a new database using Microsoft Access, there is a wizard that will ask you various questions about the new database and then will create it for you

word

two bytes of data, equivalent to sixteen bits of data

WordPad™

software utility included with Windows 95 that provides the basic functions of Microsoft Word 6. It can read and save Word 6 files and lets you format text and write complex documents.

word wrap or wraparound

system in an editing or word processing application in which the operator does not have to indicate the line endings, but can keyboard continuously, leaving the program to insert word breaks and to continue the text on the next line

workgroup

general term that refers to a collection of computers connected by a network. The workgroup would normally refer to a group of PCs that are doing similar things or within a section of a company. For example, in a magazine there might be a workgroup for the editorial journalists, another for the production department and a third for the sales department.

World Wide Web

see
WWW

worlds

three-dimensional scene that is displayed on a web site and allows a user to move around the scene exploring the objects visible; the entire scene is often called a 'world' and is created using a special plug-in extension to the web browser - often VRML
see
VRML

WORM

WRITE ONCE READ MANY TIMES MEMORY
optical disc storage system that allows the user to write data to the disc once, but the user can then read the data from the disc many times

write-back cache

temporary cache memory that will only save the information to disk or main memory when the computer instructs it to do so; this can be dangerous, since you might think that you have saved a document but it is actually stored in the write-back cache and has not been saved

write head

see
RECORD HEAD

write protect

to prevent data from being saved to a floppy disk; 3.5-inch disks have a sliding switch in the top right hand corner: if the switch is pushed down and you cannot see through the hole, then you can save data to the floppy disk, if the switch is pushed up and you can see through the hole, you cannot save data to the disk

WWW
WORLD WIDE WEB

collection of the millions of Web sites and Web pages that together form the part of the internet that is most often seen by users (although the internet also includes electronic mail, Usenet and newsgroups); each Web site is a collection of Web pages; each Web page contains text, graphics and links to other Web sites. Each page is created using the HTML language and is viewed by a user with a Web browser. To navigate between Web pages and Web sites is called surfing; this requires a computer with a link to the internet (normally using a modem) and a Web browser to view the Web pages storedd on the remote Web servers.

see also
BROWSER, CERN, HTML, INTERNET, WEB PAGE

WYSIWYG

see
WHAT YOU SEE IS WHAT YOU GET

Xx Yy Zz

X.400

CCITT standard that defines the way in which electronic mail can be transferred between different systems in a network

XA

see

CD-ROM XA

Xmodem

method of transferring files over a communications link that provides error detection features (normally using a modem over a telephone line); this method is not as fast as Zmodem because it sends smaller packets of data

XT

original version of the first IBM PC, developed by IBM, that used an 8088 processor and included a hard disk

XT keyboard

type of keyboard used with the IBM PC which had ten function keys running in two columns along the left-hand side of the keyboard. The current standard is called the AT or Windows 95 keyboard that includes 12 function keys and, in the case of a Windows 95 keyboard, a special button that's equivalent to pressing the Start button on-screen.

zero insertion force (ZIF) socket

socket on a motherboard in a computer that has movable connection terminals, allowing the chip to be inserted without using any force; a small lever is turned to grip the legs of the chip. ZIF sockets are used to hold processor chips inside your computer making it easier to replace or upgrade the processor.

zero wait state

electronic device (normally a processor or memory chip) that is fast enough to run at the same speed as the other components in a computer, so does not have to be artificially slowed down by inserting wait states

ZIF

see

ZERO INSERTION FORCE SOCKET

ZIP

filename extension given to files that contain compressed data, normally generated by the PKZIP shareware utility program

see also

COMPRESS, SELF EXTRACTING ARCHIVE

Zmodem

method of transferring files over a modem link that provides error detection and adjusts the size of each packet of data sent according to the reliability of the telephone line; if the telephone line is clear without noise, then Zmodem will send large packets of data

zoom

to enlarge an area of text or graphics (to make it easier to see or work on)

Appendix

HTML Tags

<a> .. </a>
creates a hyperlink target or source. For example, '>a href="www.pcp.co.uk">link to PCP>/a> will create a hyperlink to the PCP Web page.

<address> .. </address>
enclosed text is formatted in smaller typeface as an address

<applet> .. </applet>
defines an applet within the document

<area>
defines the area of a graphic image that will respond to a mouse click using a client-side image map

<b> .. </b>
formats enclosed text in a bold typeface

<base>
defines the URL address that is added in front of all relative URLs used within the document

<basefont>
defines the point size of the font used to format for the following text

<bgsound>
defines the audio file that is played as a background sound to the document (used in MS-IE 2 and later)

<big> .. </big>
formats enclosed text in a bigger typeface

<blockquote> .. </blockquote>
formats the enclosed text as a quotation

<body> .. </body>
defines the start and finish of this document's body text; also used to define a graphic image used as a background, and to set the default colour of the text, hyperlinks and margins for the document

**
**
inserts a line break in the text

<caption> .. </caption>
defines the caption for a table

<center> .. </center>
formats enclosed text to be centered across the line

<cite> .. </cite>
formats enclosed text as a citation

<code> .. </code>
formats enclosed text as program code, normally using the Courier typeface

<col>
defines the properties for a column that has been defined using <colgroup>; available in MS-IE 2 and above

<colgroup>
defines a column; available in MS-IE 2 and above

<comment> .. </comment>
defines the enclosed text to be a comment; only works in MS IE 2, with any other browser you should use the <!> *comment* <> tag format

<dd> .. </dd>
defines one element of a definition list

<dfn> .. </dfn>
formats enclosed text as a definition

<dir> .. </dir>
creates a directory list using the <li> to create entries

<div> .. </div>
divides the text within a document and formats each division

<dl> .. </dl>
creates a definition list using the <dd> and <dt> tags to create entries

<dt> .. </dt>
defines the definition part of an entry within a definition list

<em> .. </em>
formats enclosed text with emphasis (often the same as a bold typeface)

<embed> .. </embed>
points to an object to embed in a document

<font> .. </font>
defines the size, colour and typeface of the font to use for the enclosed text

<form> .. </form>
defines the following tags to be treated as one form; also defines how to process the form and where to send the encoded information

<frame> .. </frame>
defines a frame, including its border, colour, name and text

<frameset> .. </frameset>
defines a collection of frames

<h> .. </h>
defines a pre-set font size, such as <h1> for a large headings, <h4> for small headings

<hr>
breaks the current line of text and inserts a horizontal rule across the page

<html> .. </html>
defines the start and end of the entire html document

<i> .. </i>
formats enclosed text using an italic typeface

<iframe> .. </iframe>
defines a floating frame, used only in MS-IE 3

<img>
includes an image within a document, also defines a border for the image, size, alternative caption text and whether the image is a video clip

<input type=checkbox>
defines a checkbox button within a form

<input type=file>
defines a file-selection list within a form

<input type=image>
defines an image input element within a form

<input type=password>
defines a text input that displays an asterisk when text is entered

<input type=radio>
defines a radio button within a form

<input type=reset>
defines a button to reset the form's contents

<input type=submit>
defines a button to submit the form's contents to the named process

<input type=text>
defines a text input element to allow users to enter a line of text

<isindex>
defines the html document to be searchable by a defined search engine

<kbd> .. </kbd>
formats enclosed text as a keyboard input

<li> .. </li>
defines an item in a list; the list can be ordered using <ol> or unordered using <ul>

<link>
defines a link within a document header

<listing> .. </listing>
old tag that is the same as a the <pre> tag

<map> .. </map>
defines an image map that contains hotspots

<marquee> .. </marquee>
creates an animated scrolling text line, used in MS-IE 2 and after

<menu> .. </menu>
defines a menu that has items created using the <li> tag

<meta>
allows the programmer to include extra information about the document

<multicol> .. </multicol>
defines multiple columns within the document, used in Netscape Navigator 3 only

<nextid>
used by automated html document generators as a reference point within a file

<nobr> .. </nobr>
prevents the browser adding breaks within the enclosed text

<noframes> .. </noframes>
defines content that should be displayed if the browser does not support frames

<noscript> .. </noscript>
defines content that should be used if the browser does not support Java; only for
Netscape Navigator 3 and after

<object> .. </object>
defines an object, applet or OLE object to be inserted into the document; used for
MS-IE 3 and after

<ol> .. </ol>
defines the start and end of a numbered list; items are inserted using the <li> tag

<option> .. </option>
defines one option within a <select> tag

<p> .. </p>
defines the start and end of a paragraph

<param> .. </param>
defines the paramaters to be passed to an enclosed applet or object

<plaintext>
formats the rest of the document as plain text with spaces and breaks

<pre> .. </pre>
formats the enclosed text as plain text with spaces and breaks

<s> .. </s>
formats enclosed text with a strikethrough, horizontal line

<samp> .. </samp>
defines enclosed text as a sample

<script> .. </script>
defines the start and end of a script written in a supported language, such as JavaScript or VBScript

<select> .. </select>
defines a list of options within a form, each created using the <option> tag

<small> .. </small>
formats enclosed text in a small typesize

<spacer>
inserts a character space within a line of text; only used in Netscape Navigator 3

<span> .. </span>
define a style sheet that formats text over several tags; only used in MS-IE 3

<strike> .. </strike>
formats enclosed text with a strikethrough line

<strong> .. </strong>
formats enclosed text with emphasis, similar to bold

<style> .. </style>
defines a collection of text formatting commands that can be referred to with this style command; used for MS-IE 3 only

<sub> .. </sub>
formats enclosed text as subscript

<sup> .. </sup>
formats enclosed text as superscript

<table> .. </table>
defines a table including border, colour, size and width; columns are added with <td> and rows with <tr>

<tbody>
group of rows within a table; used in MS-IE 2

<td> .. </td>
defines a cell within a table, effectively adds a column to the table

<textarea> .. </textarea>
defines a multiple line text input element for a form

<tfoot>
defines rows within a table that are formatted as a footer to the table; used in Microsoft-IE 2

<th> .. </th>
defines the header to each column in a table

<thead>
defines rows within a table that are formatted as a header to the table; used in Microsoft-IE 2

<title> .. </title>
defines the title to this html document

<tr> .. </tr>
defines a row of cells within a table

<tt> .. </tt>
formats enclosed text in a monospaced typewrite-style font

<ul> .. </ul>
defines the start and end of a bulleted list of elements, each element is add using <li>

<var> .. </var>
enclosed text is the name of a variable

<wbr>
defines a possible point for a word break within a <nobr> line

<xmp> .. </xmp>
old tag that formats enclosed text, similar to <pre>